100 GREAT ALBUMS

First published in Great Britain in 2009 by AHS & SJS Books

www.lulu.com/greatestalbums
greatestalbums@hotmail.com

Copyright © 2009 by Andrew Southwood
The moral right of the author has been asserted

All rights reserved

No part of this publication may be reproduced, stored in a retrieval system, or transmitted in any form or by any means, without the prior permission in writing of the publisher, nor be otherwise circulated in any form of binding or cover other than that in which it is published and without a similar condition including this condition being imposed on the subsequent purchaser

A CIP catalogue record for this book is available from the British Library

ISBN: 978-0-9561547-0-5

CONTENTS

Introduction	1-4
Great Albums No 1-10	5-27
100 Great Album Tracks - Pre 1970	28-34
Great Albums No 11-34	35-75
100 Great Album Tracks 1970-79	76-81
Great Albums No 35-56	82-115
100 Great Album Tracks 1980-89	116-121
Great Albums No 57-74	122-150
100 Great Album Tracks 1990-99	151-156
Great Albums No 75-95	157-192
100 Great Album Tracks 2000-08	193-198
Great Albums No 96-100	199-206
The Greatest Albums Year-By-Year 1965-08	207-208
The Greatest Tracks Year-By-Year 1965-08	209-211
…And Finally	212-213

INTRODUCTION

In 1977 with Punk at its nihilistic height, the general consensus amongst serious album buyers was that the finest long-players had been recorded by a small group of artists primarily from the sixties. The elite consisted of the Beatles, the Rolling Stones, Bob Dylan, the Velvet Underground, Van Morrison and the Beach Boys. Of the modern heroes from the post-Aquarian age only Bruce Springsteen, Pink Floyd and Stevie Wonder were deemed architects of timeless, quality music recorded during the seventies.

By 1987 and despite the apparent upheaval that Punk generated, little seemed to have changed. The Beatles' masterpiece from 1967 remained the undisputed landmark release in the history of albums, with **Blonde On Blonde**, **Pet Sounds, Astral Weeks** and **Let It Bleed** also still considered flagships from a former age. Of the records released since 1977 few, by the late-eighties, were worthy of all-time great status, with only the debuts by the Sex Pistols and the Clash accepted as excellent examples of late-seventies rock.

Even by the late-nineties, the same classics dominated greatest albums listings. For example, the results of a poll conducted by Mojo magazine, published in January 1996, suggested that a conservative selection maintained a grip on the rock conscience of mature listeners. Making a presence in the Top 30 was only one record released in recent years, **Automatic For The People**. Equally disturbing only two albums (**The Stone Roses** and **The Queen Is Dead**), even with the benefit of maturing time and the fermenting factor crucial to so many vital records, were from the eighties.

A similar poll published in Q a couple of years later gave more reason for optimism, with a growing trend emerging. Several recent releases were serious challengers to the godly stature of the Beatles, Dylan and the Stones, with Nirvana, the Verve, Radiohead, Oasis and the Prodigy placing entries in the Top 30. However, the one observation noted from the numerous surveys over the years, including the very recent, is that the late-sixties continue to be considered the benchmark. The flower-power era has been challenged on few occasions, with the progressive early-seventies and the late-nineties proving to be worthy also-rans.

Whose opinion should we trust when deciding what qualities make a great album? After all, even respected critics can get it embarrassingly wrong. The most infamous example from modern times was the fanfare reception lavished on the 'difficult' third album by Oasis. Numerous magazines gave it top marks in their review columns, contributing to the unprecedented hype prior to its release. Disappointed record buyers soon realised when playing **Be Here Now** that the 'experts' had got it dramatically wrong. The fiasco was only one, albeit blatant, illustration of the dangers in placing too much blind faith in the valued assessments of those who sometimes have ulterior motives.

Clearly, a more reliable guide requires an opinion made with the benefit of maturity, rather than a knee-jerk reaction based on perhaps only a couple of hearings before going to press. Equally, the views of the ordinary fan rather than a professional critic may be a safer way to discover the true classics. It's with this in mind that these pages are written.

My personal collection began in 1975 (it was Queen's **A Night At The Opera**) and during the subsequent years every genre has been given a fair chance. I've never been one for pretension. Just because it's a hit with the press doesn't automatically follow for me as meaning it's a great record. I've been fooled too many times in to splashing cash on an album because the music papers gave a high recommendation. I'd like to think that the pages that follow are straight from the heart, each of the 100 albums mean the world to me.

I could so easily have got carried away, by compiling a Top 500 or, dare I say, 1000. Maybe some other time I will but, for now, I wanted to keep it compact. It wasn't an easy decision to make. Which to include and, even harder, which to leave out? I ignored compilations, on the basis that these are not albums in the true sense. Also, had I allowed for Greatest Hits etc the danger would arise of cluttering the Top 100 with career-spanning records, rather than music that captured an artist at a specific moment. The easiest decision of all, however, was electing the Number One – the greatest of all-time. It may be over forty years old and, yes, it has unavoidably dated, but no one has come close to bettering it.

(1)
SGT PEPPER'S LONELY HEARTS CLUB BAND – THE BEATLES (1967)

(*Sgt Pepper's Lonely Hearts Club Band/With A Little Help From My Friends/Lucy In The Sky With Diamonds/Getting Better/Fixing A Hole/She's Leaving Home/Being For The Benefit Of Mr Kite/Within You Without You/When I'm Sixty-Four/Lovely Rita/Good Morning Good Morning/Sgt Pepper's Lonely Hearts Club Band (Reprise)/A Day In The Life*)

Top Track: *A Day In The Life*

An early insight came by way of the double A-Side 45, *Penny Lane/Strawberry Fields Forever*. The former was Paul McCartney's story-telling pop at its best, reaching the top of the US chart but no one really knew what to make of the latter. Rather than sing, John Lennon narrated his way through a series of inconsequential lyrics. They made little sense (unless you were stoned), whilst musically strayed far from the safe, melodic formula that the world had grown to love. Further notoriety followed when the single failed to top the UK charts, their first release not to do so since *Please Please Me* in early 1963. It doesn't matter anymore - the combination of sugar-sweet pop with weird experimentalism has, over time, warmed to subsequent generations, with these two songs now regarded amongst the greatest 45s ever. During the early months of 1967 the world realised the Beatles were crafting something special.

The historic moment when the album became more important than the single occurred in June 1967, with the release of ***Sgt Pepper's Lonely Hearts Club Band***. For the band it represented the culmination of their musical aspirations since August 1966, when they performed their final live concert in front of a packed audience at Candlestick Park, San Francisco. Tired of singing songs that few could hear due to screaming fans, the Fab

Four retreated to the safety of the recording studio and concentrated on writing new material.

Just over three months later they began the first sessions for the new album and yet, by the spring of 1967 were still creating the final touches. In comparison with their usual rapid recording output, the time being afforded was epic (their debut released in 1963 was produced in a matter of days). Rock was evidently moving to unexplored territory and even the Beatles could no longer instantaneously conjure-up magic. Nevertheless, rumours were rife that they were recording a masterpiece to excel its predecessor. When the point of truth arrived, few were disappointed.

Renowned critic, Kenneth Tynan, was so impressed that he described the new record as 'a decisive moment in Western civilisation'. **Sgt Pepper's Lonely Hearts Club Band** was an entirely unique experience. Simply by picking up the LP cover the listener could sense that this was no ordinary album. The sleeve contained a collage of famous characters, many from popular entertainment including Laurel and Hardy, Marilyn Monroe, Bob Dylan and, yes, the Fab Four. The fact that the Beatles were included illustrated the point being made that this was a record performed by another group, the fictitious Sgt Pepper.

The LP came in a gatefold cover, which in itself wasn't unusual, the difference this time, however, was that this wasn't a double album. So why use a cover normally reserved for housing two records? All was soon revealed. One sleeve contained the vinyl, whilst in the other could be found a piece of cardboard displaying pictures ready to be cut out. How many people snipped out their moustache, picture card, military stripes, badges and stand-up picture of the Sgt Pepper Band will never be known, but it can be imagined that caught up in all the excitement, thousands of scissors sliced in to cardboard during the hazy summer of '67.

A colourful photograph of the make-believe group adorned the inside sleeve, remarkably looking like the Beatles. The back cover also broke new ground by providing the song lyrics, nicely typed, ready for the whole world to start singing. With fake moustache glued to upper lip, badges and stripes pinned to the arms and lyric sheet to hand, the only thing remaining was to put the record on. 'A splendid time is guaranteed for all' - it said so on the back sleeve. From the opening chords by an orchestra tuning-up through to the eternal fading away of the final track, Sgt Pepper delivered its promise.

The presence of chemical assistance to generate this pleasure became obvious, with laughable public attention focusing on *Lucy In The Sky With Diamonds* (LSD). It presumably had taken tremendous imagination or 'something' to devise a vision of strange coloured trees and skies, but can we imagine a world today without this song's imaginative lyrics? It made for a nice story to believe that this stunningly original composition was inspired by hallucinogenic activity, but Lennon admitted it was a child's painting that provided the cue for enigmatic lyrics.

Drug references, nevertheless, were found elsewhere and in abundance - *Fixing A Hole*, for example, left little to the imagination. *A Day In The Life* with its mind-blowing inferences clearly dwelled on a drugged existence. For a while, radio stations around the globe felt uneasy about broadcasting the song, more concerned about upsetting their regular listeners than appreciating the greatest track on an album that changed everything. That the pivotal man in the story may have come from the House of Lords, only added fuel to the growing controversy.

For those that understood the plot, Sgt Pepper was acknowledged for the quality of many innovative songs, advanced production techniques and for its brave ambition to push the limits. Many, slow in realising the enormity of the occasion, failed to comprehend, wanting nothing more than for the group to resume singing simplistic tunes. For them, a return to the innocence of *She Loves You* wasn't to be. The days of the Beatles touring and writing snappy pop odes were gone forever. A brave new world had been born and the Beatles were the chief instigators.

Even on a definitive LP like this, there were still flawed cuts that raised eyebrows. *Within You Without You* is often seen as the weak link and, at over five minutes, tends to outstay its welcome. The inclusion of this lengthy ode to Eastern religious philosophy, on a record where the objective centred on creating a masterpiece of discovery, was a courageous decision. Subsequent technology means that the listener can programme the CD to skip it but doing so completely misses the point. The crux of the matter rests on Sgt Pepper being the first concept album of the rock era. Some songs in isolation seem unplayable but, as if by magic, listen to them in the order that they appear on the LP and everything fits perfectly into place.

It has to be heard in its entirety, for the journey it travels is the finest aural delight ever. From the opening title-track and onwards to *Getting Better, She's Leaving Home, Lovely Rita* and outwards to *A Day In The Life*, rock has never felt so good and will probably not better the standards set.

(2)

REVOLVER – THE BEATLES (1966)

(*Taxman/Eleanor Rigby/I'm Only Sleeping/Love You To/Here, There And Everywhere/Yellow Submarine/She Said She Said/Good Day Sunshine/And Your Bird Can Sing/For No One/Dr Robert/I Want To Tell You/Got To Get You Into My Life/Tomorrow Never Knows*)

Top Track: Tomorrow Never Knows

Having conquered the world between 1962-66 with a string of groundbreaking albums and singles, the Beatles reached a major crossroads. Live concerts increasingly became farcical events, tarnished by hysterical, screaming fans drowning the band's performance. Equally, popular audience demand for a regurgitation of earlier hits threatened to stifle their quest for creativeness. By the summer of '66 society had changed significantly from that of '63. In turn, the loveable mop tops that sang an innocent ode to romance, *I Want To Hold Your Hand*, now preferred hallucinogenic pleasures.

Their decision to quit touring was an easy one to make. In doing so, it allowed for more capacity in the recording studio, with manoeuvrability towards experimentation. Advanced dividends from this stance were noted earlier in the year, on *Paperback Writer* b/w *Rain*, but it was **Revolver** (recorded April-June '66) that truly signalled their intent.

Critics and fans will forever debate the merits of this masterpiece versus its landmark successor. Which of these two records has survived the ravages of time the best? It remains the closest call in rock's history. Numerous polls have been published over the years, and invariably the Beatles justifiably jostle for the top two slots. For some, the concept LP from 1967 steals the show, for others it is marred by excessive psychedelic infringements, leaving an undesirable date stamp. Whichever way, the two complement each other so well they are unquestionably rock's greatest albums.

Taxman represented a seismic shift in George Harrison's song-writing skills. Could it really be that this was the same man that a year before contributed *I Need You* to **Help!** and *Think For Yourself* to **Rubber Soul**, both low points on their respective sets? *Taxman* also upheld the band's talent for creating lyrics that ordinary folk could empathise with. The same could be said for *Eleanor Rigby*, surely the loneliest lady in the world. For sure, the Beatles had explored themes of abject loneliness before but never with such tangible teardrop emotion. Screeching violins, a riveting storyline (spotlighting McCartney's economical lyricism) and a tune to die for, it was a 2:07 minutes gem in defining pop.

I'm Only Sleeping, with its bizarre backward playing guitar solos and hazy, slumbering production, reflected John Lennon's love for lengthy snoozes, although quick-off-the-mark commentators searched for drug-induced messages within the lyrics. Sitars were heard in 1965 but *Love You To* placed Harrison's fascination for

Indian religion and musical instruments firmly in focus. It felt so clumsy, his vocals characteristically peppered by a Merseyside accent, in an uncomfortable union with twangy, foreign-string 'noises'. Yet, it worked! It was a similar peculiarity with *Yellow Submarine*. On any other LP such a silly, throwaway tune would have been awful. On **Revolver**, sandwiched in between the vulnerably sweet *Here, There And Everywhere* and the spiralling mania of *She Said She Said* it was cartoon, bubblegum pop happily at home.

The formerly uniformed group were now showing signs of splintering within their united exterior. Whereas McCartney upheld pop sensibility (*Good Day Sunshine*, *For No One* and *Got To Get You Into My Life*) and Harrison wrestled with his fledgling interest in mystical faith, it was Lennon that made courageous steps towards the unknown. *Dr Robert* was littered with drug references, whilst the high-octane *And Your Bird Can Sing* was synonymous with the music scene's transition from pop to rock. Nothing though, could prepare anyone for the final three minutes to an album embracing pop, soul, psychedelic rock, Eastern spiritualism and unhealthy Western influences.

Lennon's original plan for *Tomorrow Never Knows* was to incorporate chanting monks, but evidently this was unworkable within the restraints of a recording studio. Instead, a sequence of looped tapes, reversed instrumentation and hypnotic drum beats supported his 'strange' yarns (allegedly inspired by The Tibetan Book Of The Dead and The Psychedelic Experience). It began with an invitation to switch off your mind and float away, but less than 180 seconds later Lennon's mesmerising mini-epic successfully span rock's axle, speeding the genre towards distant boundaries. The whole experience could be summarised with just one word – weird. Popular music had heard nothing like it. To think that the Beatles concluded **Help!** with a cover-version of *Dizzy Miss Lizzy* – the times they certainly were a-changin'.

(3)
NEVERMIND – NIRVANA (1991)

(Smells Like Teen Spirit/In Bloom/Come As You Are/Breed/Lithium/Polly/Territorial Pissings/Drain You/ Lounge Act/Stay Away/On A Plain/Something In The Way/Endless Nameless)

Top Track: Smells Like Teen Spirit

Nirvana's debut, **Bleach**, was allegedly recorded on a budget of $600 and, it has to be said, the sound quality reflected the low economy. This was never going to be anything other than an abrasive production but despite the obvious drawbacks, the music holds up well to scrutiny. It was like a mythical Year Zero again, as key tracks *Love Buzz*, *Down* and *About A Girl* revealed a template that ultimately placed them at the forefront of US rock. Enough promise could be found to encourage Geffen to offer Nirvana a contract. When the follow-up, **Nevermind**, hit the shops in late 1991 the record company's decision was handsomely rewarded.

The video to the lead single, *Smells Like Teen Spirit*, benefited from saturation airplay on MTV, swiftly installing the band as the new champions and, some would say, saviours of rock. The video primarily focused on Kurt Cobain peering into the camera, hair ruffled, half-sneering and snarling his way through lyrics that soon developed legendary status. Disillusioned kids in the audience, boredom sketched on their faces, reacted by jumping with liberation to their feet and started dancing like US teenagers hadn't done since the sixties.

There is no question that this riff-heavy song is ultra-important in rock history, but some nagging doubts linger surrounding its complete originality. Did Nirvana borrow riffs from Boston's *More Than A Feeling*? Yes, there are slight similarities but it's an identifiably common problem for musicians to always be original, as Cobain subsequently confessed during *On A Plain*. Whether *Smells Like Teen Spirit* was a 100% original piece of work or slightly borrowed would, as time passed, become a redundant concern. For now, dejected youth had a hero in whom they could relate - the so called Generation X had been born.

Much in common with the Grunge movement, Nirvana's influences were readily evident. Anyone familiar with Black Sabbath during the period when Ozzy fronted the band identified them as a major inspiration source, coupled with a healthy obsession with Punk/New Wave. The collision between Punk and vintage rock was never more apparent than on *Lithium*, with its wonderful use/borrowing/ pilfering of the loud-quiet-loud technique perfected by Sabbath in 1973 on **Sabbath Bloody Sabbath**. Cobain declared he was happy on this song thanks to friends in his head but in truth he was far from it, his disposition to a depressive state aggravated by the conflicting struggles of fame and fortune, whilst yearning privacy. *Lithium* was a simplification of the album, characterised by wild mood swings swaying randomly from gentle to aggressive, with little room for compromise.

On *Territorial Pissings* it was pure maximum adrenalin Punk all the way as Cobain prophetically shrieked his desire for escape. Elsewhere could be found sedate acoustic numbers, providing shelter from the storm, notably on the two bookends that closed sides one and two (vinyl/cassette versions), *Polly* and *Something In The Way*. Technically the latter wasn't the last composition - that annoying by-product of the CD, the hidden track, resulted on this occasion in a fifteen minutes wait. When it did eventually arrive the delay wasn't worth it, the style of the song being out of step with the credited tracks. Nothing more than guitar feedback and howling by Cobain, its absence from the title credits was only too appropriate in name also, *Endless Nameless*.

In just a few weeks Nirvana were thrust from nowhere towards a global stage, with media interest attracted to the lead singer. Cobain found fame difficult to handle. Falling into the same trap that snared so many icons before him, he became entangled with drugs. From there onwards his life spiralled hopelessly beyond control, culminating in tragedy in April 1994. Speculation and conspiracy theorists dwelled over the album's first three songs with their lyrical references to guns. Despite his assurances on *Come As You Are* that he didn't possess a gun, as dramatic events unfolded in 1994 the truth concerning his relationship with the weapon took a sinister twist. In the wake of **Nevermind** new bands sprang up overnight trying to emulate the Nirvana sound, oblivious that it had existed for years already, only in two different camps.

If the rock yarn about the Velvet Underground's debut is true, that everyone who bought it wanted to form their own band, then Nirvana came a close second as creators of one of the most influential albums. Sound-alikes were everywhere but none matching the ferocity and excitement heard on *Smells Like Teen Spirit, Stay Away, Breed* and *On A Plain*.

(4)

NEVER MIND THE BOLLOCKS HERE'S THE SEX PISTOLS – SEX PISTOLS (1977)

(Holidays In The Sun/Bodies/Liar/No Feelings/God Save The Queen/Problems/Seventeen/Anarchy In The UK/ Submission/Pretty Vacant/New York/EMI)

Top Track: Anarchy In The UK

The key moment from 1976 was the opening shot fired by the Sex Pistols - *Anarchy In The UK*. Its title alone unsettled a nervous Establishment, threatened in recent years by nothing more harrowing than men wearing lipstick with girly haircuts. With just one sweeping statement, the band put the shock back in rock. This was music that your parents hated, your younger brothers and sisters couldn't comprehend and which the complacent rock scene initially failed to appreciate. At last, the seventies generation had something to brag about.

The Sex Pistols lived in an alternative universe to conventional rock, symbolised by ripped jeans, abundant swearing and an absolute hatred for everything. They also set out to d-e-s-t-r-o-y-y-y-y... Right from the start it was obvious that *Anarchy In The UK* was no ordinary 45. The song was considered by some as an incitement to the nation's youth to take protest to the streets, whilst others saw it for what it really was – paramount to the Second Coming. With its thought-provoking comments and references to the M.P.L.A, U.D.A. and I.R.A, rock's voice as a vehicle through which to channel political views had returned. *God Save The Queen* followed in its controversial footsteps by drawing comparisons between the monarch and a fascist regime, concluding with Johnny Rotten's classic sign-off that the Queen had no future.

Despite the familiarity of three singles on the LP prior to its release (*Pretty Vacant* was the third), hearing **Never Mind The Bollocks Here's The Sex Pistols** for the first time was earth-shattering, life-defining. From the opening feet-stamping *Holidays In The Sun* (the fourth 45), the bloody and shocking *Bodies* (a tale of a girl with an aborted foetus in a carrier-bag), through to the closing *EMI* (sticking two-fingers up, plus a raspberry, to their former record company), music had rarely felt so violent. To the observant, the album took on greater significance. This was nothing less than Britain's declaration of independence, after recent years of US dominance by AOR. It came, ironically, via an American concept that embraced stripped to basics rock and most importantly, with bags of that vital ingredient - attitude.

Over thirty years since its release, the adrenalin surge that kicks off *Holidays In The Sun* still sends shivers down the spine, the spiteful hatred spitting from *Liar* and *No Feelings* induce palpitations and that revolution in the air buzz on *Anarchy In The UK* makes hairs stand on end. It was apparent that this set carried an important message that MUST be heard - true in 1977 and, more so today. These twelve songs didn't just change the future direction of rock they saved it from premature death. Those that get excited at the prospects of standing next to a detonator will understand the utter relevance of this LP. Sense the danger, feel the heat, touch lethal electrification of the spirit - it doesn't get more explosive than this.

(5)
CLOSER – JOY DIVISION (1980)

(*Atrocity Exhibition/Isolation/Passover/Colony/A Means To An End/Heart And Soul/Twenty Four Hours/The Eternal/Decades*)

Top Track: Atrocity Exhibition

In May 1980 the lead singer of Britain's most critically acclaimed act from the post-Punk era committed suicide. Whilst his epilepsy and entrenched depression were common knowledge, few realised the full extent of his internal despair. In his darkest hour and despite the numbing of emotional anguish by alcohol, Ian Curtis could take no more, bringing his tormented life to a sad conclusion.

Valuable insight, and perhaps explanations, for his personal collapse were available by listening to Joy Division's second LP, **Closer**. Released shortly after his death, it inevitably interested the grave-digging theorists searching for clues in 'revealing' lyrics. They didn't need to look far to uncover warning-signs of a man suffering from intense turmoil. In particular *Atrocity Exhibition*, *A Means To An End* and *Twenty Four Hours* arguably suggested a pre-destined tragedy.

The music revolved around subdued vocals, delivered with a haunting agony not heard since Jim Morrison's crazed exploits. Fittingly *Decades* seemingly pointed towards the Californian hero, with an emphasis on delving through the darkest depths of hell. Like Morrison before, Curtis lost control, his self-destruction an unavoidable consequence of fixation with the dark side.

Once again, a talented star took to the grave answers to enticing questions. What if he hadn't died, his mental health miraculously recovered and further work followed? What music would Joy Division have made in the mid-eighties? Or did New Order provide the answer to this? A lasting legacy exists with **Closer** –

the loneliest, bleakest but, paradoxically, life-enriching album of all-time. Guilt, shame, rejection and isolation were prominent, the lyrics transfixed by impending doom.

Although a sombre moodiness hovers throughout, there were occasional bouts of uplifting musical relief, notably on *Heart And Soul* (the missing link between the Doors and the Stone Roses?), *Isolation* and *A Means To An End*. Not, however, a first choice for a night of celebrations but most definitely one that offers intriguing visions, reflecting painful thoughts from an intensely troubled mind.

(6)

DARK SIDE OF THE MOON – PINK FLOYD (1973)

(*Speak To Me/Breathe/On The Run/Time/The Great Gig In The Sky/Money/Us And Them/Any Colour You Like/ Brain Damage/Eclipse*)

Top Track: Time

Dark Side Of The Moon is often viewed as the ultimate headphone-album and when listening to it with cans on it's easy to understand why. Over the course of 43 minutes a series of inter-linked songs, layered by heart beats, chiming clocks, cash registers and intermittent, inconsequential conversations ricocheted from one ear to the other.

Beginning in total silence, gradually a faint heartbeat became audible, a muttering voice appeared, feeding through to the first song 'proper', *Breathe*. Continuing the recent rock tradition for concept albums, the agenda for Pink Floyd covered madness and death, ignited by modern day lifestyle pressures, with its inherent necessity to rush around from A to B and back again. Work, work and more work is for most of us all that life seems to be about - no wonder that so many related to its meaningful lyrics.

Contemporary life is a constant race against the clock but surely nothing compares with the frantic footsteps, running to get somewhere on the synthesiser rush, *On The Run*. So much puffing and panting, the sweat could virtually be felt dripping off the face. Was that rushing worth it in the end, as the sounds of a crash brought the track to a dramatic conclusion? The explosive booms resulting from the disaster slowly subsided, to be 'out-noised' by the gentle ticking of clocks. Coming so soon after manic energy, the shift in pace couldn't have been more extreme. Then, it was enough to test the calmest nerves, as though in a possessed jeweller's store, every demonic clock began chiming. Anyone playing the LP for the first time whilst wearing headphones would surely be in need for a tonic - alcoholic or chemical. Fortunately, a musical solution came in the shape of the album's centrepiece, *Time*.

The idea of growing old, just a little too quickly, is something that strikes a recognisable chord. Life can be miserable and mundane, where if we're not careful, the most precious thing passes by and before we know it, it's too late. During the innocence of youth it would be disturbing to think that the days were passing by too fast. Then as we get older, weeks, months and years propel away from us in the fading sunset. The song's lyrics said everything about this emotive issue, but adding a thrilling texture, came one of those awesome guitar solos for which David Gilmour remains worshipped as a rock god. Side 1 concluded with guest vocalist, Clare Torry, displaying a good time without speaking any words. *The Great Gig In The Sky* it was called, but more earthly pleasures were noted - the closest music's been to capturing an orgasm and putting it on vinyl.

Money, released as a 45, became a minor hit in America where its radio-friendly appeal helped boost album sales. A venomous song, fuelled by anger and blunt-talking, in some respects it also came across as being a poke at themselves and the industry they were unwillingly becoming locked into. The relaxing atmosphere generated by *Us And Them* almost hid the moral tale of injustice during the Great War, when millions died and for what? A fortunate few were not subjected to 'going over the top' (Them), whilst the lower/working classes (Us) were looked upon as having no value attached to their lives. Above all, this track complete with a theme simultaneously focused on paranoia, was complemented by a superb saxophone solo by Dick Parry.

Less traditional instruments were used on the synthesiser instrumental paradise *Any Colour You Like*, before modern lifestyle anxieties returned for the penultimate, *Brain Damage*. The lunatic began on the grass (the lawn or smoke?), then menacingly moved towards the hall and in to the head. It was about break-ups and cracking-ups. It was also impossibly simplistic and yet so totally captivating.

Dark Side Of The Moon was one of the definitive markers during the seventies, displaying a new peak in recording excellence and showing how good progressive rock could get. Those subsequently purchasing the CD version still had the printed lyrics included, but missed out on the other surprises received with the vinyl all those years ago. The freebies inside the LP cover featured stickers and two posters (one picturing the band, the other of the Egyptian pyramids mysteriously in blue).

The CD update replicated the stickers and posters inside the jewel case but it wasn't quite the same. Somehow, trying to stick a shrunken to size picture of Pink Floyd and the pyramids on a bedroom wall was plain silly. Also, unlike with vinyl, on the reverse side of the pictures could be found the lyrics, making it a not too difficult decision as to whether the mini-posters should go anywhere, other than back in their case. Even after several years, this album still sounds as if it had been recorded only last week, with recent polls suggesting it will remain a firm favourite with rock fans.

(7)

ASTRAL WEEKS – VAN MORRISON (1968)

(Astral Weeks/Beside You/Sweet Thing/Cyprus Avenue/ The Way Young Lovers Do/Madame George/Ballerina/Slim Slow Slider)

Top Track: Astral Weeks

Northern Ireland band, Them, achieved limited success during the mid-sixties, despite releasing the highly-influential singles *Here Comes The Night* and *Gloria*. With musical differences blamed for their demise front man, Van Morrison, seized the opportunity to pursue his talents, keen to work on music that veered away from pop. During 1967 he signed an ill-fated contract with the Bang label, agreeing to a series of sessions. Regrettably, it was a relationship ill at ease, the aspirations of the company at odds with what Morrison desired. Ironically, he scored a sizeable hit 45 with *Brown Eyed Girl*, a saccharine-overdosed tune that shared little resemblance with the man. In his mind's eye there existed a strong ambition, reaching fruition the following year. During September 1968, he entered a recording studio in New York and within a few weeks completed his masterpiece - **Astral Weeks**.

Warner Brothers producer, Lewis Merenstein, gathered a cast of musicians that included Connie Kay and Richard Davis from the Modern Jazz Quartet, and John Payne, Jay Berliner and Warren Smith, all seasoned N.Y. session players. However, to those concerned, Morrison represented an unknown quantity, with a reputation founded on his brief period with Them and an erratic solo career. Little was known of the compositions that he brought with him to the studio.

On paper it didn't make for a promising proposition and, given the music's complexity, it would surely take time for everyone to familiarise themselves with the structures. Despite the obvious drawbacks of such a spontaneous assembly, a tremendous bonding of musical talent emerged. Indeed, the most memorable aspect of the album has been the sense of mutual respect and admiration amongst accomplished musicians, shining through with generous warmth. There was an overwhelming feeling of togetherness, as if these guys had played together for years, with an artistic appreciation of the intricacies of Morrison's vision.

In reality, the musical arrangements were little more than improvisations, lengthy and sprawling, strengthened by a curious delving into traditional Irish Folk, US Blues and contemporary Jazz. The eight songs flowed with a continuous current, a rock opera as Morrison preferred to describe them. What he sang about sometimes bordered on bewildering, but his enthralling meanderings, especially on *Cyprus Avenue* and his unrelenting love for a *Ballerina* were impossibly endearing. Above all, a spiritual world presence prevailed, portraying the dark and desolate streets of Belfast as a poetically romantic paradise.

Although critics rave over the nine-minute excellence of *Madame George* and the Blues purity found in *Cyprus Avenue*, it was the title-track that warrants undiluted praise. It contained one of the most crucial bass lines ever to grace a record, accompanying a hypnotic tale with higher-ground lyrics. For over seven minutes *Astral Weeks*, with transcendental cryptic messages and haunting, stringed orchestrations, laid the glorious foundations for the seven mystical cuts that followed in its path. Long before 'fusion' was used to tag a form of music encompassing varying styles, Morrison already mastered the art-form, entwining Folk, Blues and Jazz, with ghostly imagery from Gaelic heritage.

Once again, an album worthy of huge public acclaim fell on deaf ears. A crucial factor in its disappointing commercial impact was the absence of 45s, and with good reason. Unlike the charming *Brown Eyed Girl*, **Astral Weeks** contained nothing remotely palatable to a pop audience. Joe Smith (Vice-President of Warner

Brothers) suggested to Morrison that the LP would possibly be a steady seller for about six years. Over forty years later it still moderately sells, with a new, younger audience picking-up on its fascinating mysticism. A classic amongst classics, this record is highly recommended - those looking for an introduction to Van Morrison should start here.

(8)

BLONDE ON BLONDE – BOB DYLAN (1966)

(*Rainy Day Women #12 & 35/Pledging My Time/Visions Of Johanna/One Of Us Must Know (Sooner Or Later)/I Want You/Stuck Inside Of Mobile With The Memphis Blues Again/Leopard-Skin Pill-Box Hat/Just Like A Woman/Most Likely You Go Your Way (And I'll Go Mine)/Temporary Like Achilles/Absolutely Sweet Marie/Fourth Time Around/ Obviously Five Believers/Sad Eyed Lady Of The Lowlands*)

Top Track: Visions Of Johanna

Whereas the key Brit Invasion bands, in tandem with the Beach Boys, re-set the definitions of a great album via sugar-coated pop, Dylan careered his own path towards the same goal. His twin landmark releases in 1965 catapulted Folk towards uncomfortable terrain, causing puritans to question his commitment to the genre. Accusations were levied that his 'conversion' to rock constituted the ultimate betrayal, reaching a symbolic peak when a disgruntled fan, during a performance at the Manchester Free Trade Hall in May 1966, yelled 'Judas!'. It was a moment of instantaneous folklore but did little to dissuade Dylan from channelling his Woody Guthrie/Beatnik vision for Folk music, by taking it towards a commercial domain. His panoramic scope prompted a prolific creative output, culminating in the double LP, **Blonde On Blonde**.

Released during the same month as **Pet Sounds**, Dylan's tour de force adventure could not have been further removed from the Beach Boys and their sunset harmonies. It was lauded as a major milestone in rock development, touted as the first great double LP, but you wouldn't have thought so on being greeted by the introductory *Rainy Day Women #12 & 35*. Here was a song that sounded as though the backing band were still warming-up, a whimsical send-up, with Dylan's vocals almost mocking serious belief, but make no mistake about it – a nomadic, bohemian journey was about to begin.

Pledging My Time marks the true starting point for what, there onwards, was a faultless set of immense proportions. In comparison with his earlier releases, **Blonde On Blonde** was a reservoir bursting with material suitable for radio-friendly airplay, with no fewer than five tracks (across US/UK charts) culled for 45 status. It was, however, away from the spotlight of commercial considerations that his best compositions lay.

For every upbeat *Stuck Inside Of Mobile With The Memphis Blues Again* and *Absolutely Sweet Marie*, equilibrium was emphatically maintained via restrained drama, typically on the highpoint *Visions Of Johanna* and *Temporary Like Achilles*. The former alluded to the presence of 'someone' but, despite the apparent clue offered in the name, the lyrics were teasingly ambiguous, providing the inquisitive with a raft of possible candidates. Dylan's spaced-out, somewhat lethargic, deliverance of his words hinted to some at a drugs-connection, heightened by characters within the song cryptically referring to various substances. In essence, regardless of who or what the subject matter, it was simply his second best track ever.

The double vinyl space allowed him to expand on previous ideas tested on earlier albums, reaching an epic scale on the mammoth *Sad Eyed Lady Of The Lowlands* spanning the entire length of Side 4 (admittedly, at 11:23 minutes, a further track to bolster the final vinyl slice would not have gone amiss). Even so, this isolated song finds Dylan's story-telling cruising into overdrive, structured around five stanzas using a female character, reportedly his wife, Sara, as the focal point.

You have to look at this LP in context. 1966 was still a time of relative innocence, when 45s were invariably comprised of contrived romantic verses, confined within a three-minutes time frame. Long-players remained a haphazard mechanism for bolting songs together, rather than a serious medium through which to express a wider opinion. Within the Folk music world the boundaries were even more rigid, with a pre-set hostility to exploration of its parameters. With this in mind, **Blonde On Blonde** was light years ahead of the field, second only to **Revolver** in the pre-Summer Of Love releases.

(9)

LED ZEPPELIN IV (1971)

(*Black Dog/Rock 'n' Roll/The Battle Of Evermore/Stairway To Heaven/Misty Mountain Hop/Four Sticks/Going To California/When The Levee Breaks*)

Top Track: Stairway To Heaven

Undeterred by the backlash encountered on the release of their third album, accused by purists for going soft, Led Zeppelin continued to pursue their love for Folk music. On first listening to their fourth set initial thoughts, however, were that they had completely abandoned the lighter texture prevalent on their preceding LP. **Led Zeppelin IV** opened with the thundering, perfect for air-guitar assault *Black Dog*, on which Robert Plant showcased the full range of his menacing voice. Together with the bombardment from John Bonham, John Paul Jones and Jimmy Page the song was a breath-taking experience – stunning but pleasantly exhausting.

Next up and defying the laws of logic, they increased the pace further, on the supersonic *Rock 'n' Roll*. Once again, coming to the fore were the talents of each member, further welcome commitment to their powerful force that distinguished them from all others. Plant bordered on losing complete control, Page and Jones were in healthy competition to see who could play the fastest and then there was Bonham, reliable as ever, pounding the drums into annihilated submission.

After two rock-based tracks a change in pace, even for those that were outraged at the going-soft on the third album, came as welcome relief. Song three, *The Battle Of Evermore*, drastically altered the complexion. Suddenly, the thunder from the opening booms died away and there was only silence. Then, fading in ever so slightly, the gentle sound of a mandolin incited an air of uncertainty, before Plant and (good grief on a Zeppelin album) a woman began to sing. This lady, however, was none other than one of England's finest in Sandy Denny. *The Battle Of Evermore* relayed a bizarre story that could have fallen out of a chapter from Tolkien's Lord Of The Rings. Its placing on the LP initially felt peculiar, being better matched to its predecessor. Nevertheless, it served to slow the tempo, ushering in the mystical glory that would bring the shutters down on Side One.

For some time the band had shown that there were two sides to their chemistry; a blow-the-speakers-off-the-wall metallic mentality versus pastoral Folk tones. It was only a matter of time before these two aspects were welded together, within the same song, and with awesome results. Evidence existed in previous attempts, decisive warnings heard on *Ramble On* (**Led Zeppelin II**) and *Babe I'm Gonna Leave You* (**Led Zeppelin**), where the soft acoustics caved in under a barrage of explosive electric carnage. On the third LP the polarised themes were on the whole kept apart, making it noticeable that there was a softer touch. It seemed **Led Zeppelin IV** was going down the same path, by keeping separate these contrasting formulas, but then along came the fourth track and a place in history. At long last, Led Zeppelin masterfully fused their two chief inspiration sources, unleashing a monster of popular music - an anthem that for years has topped opinion polls as the best album track of all-time.

Stairway To Heaven drew attention before the vinyl even reached the turntable, due to its printed lyrics on the inner sleeve. The inside cover featured a drawing of a young woman, looking upwards at a giant, bearded old man holding a lantern, with a bright star shining from within. What was the purpose to this drawing? The song's opening segment offered no clues. It was nothing jaw-dropping, just a straightforward acoustic guitar delicately handled. Then Plant began narrating the tale of a lady, with a string of mystical messages that were open to translation in numerous ways.

The listener by now intrigued, would be attentively following the lyrics, although what could be made of them has constantly been a source of argument. It lasted close to the eight minutes mark, building in pace gradually, the mood became more upbeat, optimism filled the air - the world was a nicer place to live. The peak came as Plant took a break from the lengthy song sheet and Page stepped in to perform one of rock's most celebrated guitar solos. Barely a minute later Plant resumed from where he left off, but what an incredulous experience! The tempo increased to all-out speed, before winding down until *Stairway To Heaven* concluded with a whimper. A song of hope and rousing emotions, rock had reached a new zenith.

Side Two maintained a similar format to the first. *Misty Mountain Hop* and *Four Sticks* were heads down rockers followed by the slower, acoustic hippy-ideology of *Going To California*. The closing song, *When The Levee Breaks*, tends to be overlooked because of its more famous bed-fellows. It featured fewer lyrics and sounded less commercial but arguably it encapsulated the band's hard rock ethos – visualise Delta Blues crushed by a contemporary attitude and you'll get the picture. Rightly so, co-authorship was credited to Memphis Minnie. **Led Zeppelin IV** was their career best.

(10)
THE JOSHUA TREE – U2 (1987)

(Where The Streets Have No Name/I Still Haven't Found What I'm Looking For/With Or Without You/Bullet The Blue Sky/ Running To Stand Still/Red Hill Mining Town/In God's Country/Trip Through Your Wires/One Tree Hill/ Exit/Mothers Of The Disappeared)

Top Track: Where The Streets Have No Name

The CD era's first major milestone release came from U2 with a widescreen vision of their big obsession, Americana. One glimpse at the cover to **The Joshua Tree**, picturing them standing in the middle of a desert, left no doubts that this was going to be a red-hot affair. The music matched this molten tension with an equal level of sizzling heat that showed capability of scorching vinyl (there were music fans out there still buying the 12" black things).

The opening cut, *Where The Streets Have No Name*, appeared intent on resuming from where *MLK* had concluded on **The Unforgettable Fire**. It was as though U2 were harbouring desires on Pink Floyd circa 1975 but, by song's end, the pace accelerated to full throttle, punctuated by lyrical connections to high temperatures. *I Still Haven't Found What I'm Looking For* captured the band philosophising, seeking redemption and searching for solutions. The surprise lead single, *With Or Without You*, wasn't an obvious choice, due to its venomous adherence to bitter love. It was, however, a quintessential 'grower' that in time justified its role.

Momentum increased on the tense, disturbing *Bullet The Blue Sky* - you could almost choke on the smouldering smoke from blazes caused by fallen bombs (the song had originally been inspired by US involvement in the El Salvador Civil War in the early-eighties). The Edge revealed an awesome technique halfway through, simulating sirens whilst Bono observed military planes flying over mud huts. If the passive listener remained in two minds as to the album's focus of environment, then *Running To Stand Still* (troubled musing over heroin addiction) settled it. With tracks reflecting on drug abuse, religious yearning and warfare, the sweat poured off the skin from just listening to the first half of **The Joshua Tree**.

The old time America theme continued onwards, with *Red Hill Mining Town* and *In God's Country*. The latter was so brief but made a bigger impact than many songs twice its length. In only 2:57 minutes the aural passenger was launched on a rapid journey (through Ireland or the US?), only to be promptly chucked out with no prior warning. Poignancy arrived with *One Tree Hill*, a tribute to poet Greg Caroll, the funeral of whom the band attended at Wanganui, New Zealand on 10 July 1986.

The difficult final offering, *Mothers Of The Disappeared*, relayed the story of mothers who lost children during the military dictatorship in Chile during the seventies. It indicated U2's growing commitment to pass comment on political issues and with more authority than on previous occasions. Such was their sincerity to the cause of speaking-up on behalf of those afraid or being prevented from doing so, Amnesty International's address was printed alongside the lyric sheet, three times - for Ireland, Britain and America. It was so very eighties but, at the time, it seemed totally appropriate.

The Joshua Tree worked on many levels. Not only did it show the creativeness of producer Daniel Lanois in partnership with Brian Eno, it also lifted U2's stature as an intellectual force. Further evidence, if it were needed, that they were hitting peaks, was found in the quality of the B-Sides (vinyl) to the singles. The most famous flip side from their mighty output, *The Sweetest Thing*, a decade later was dusted down, polished and became a UK Number 1.

100 GREAT ALBUM TRACKS – PRE 1970

1. LIKE A ROLLING STONE (**HIGHWAY 61 REVISITED**) – BOB DYLAN 1965
2. TOMORROW NEVER KNOWS (**REVOLVER**) – THE BEATLES 1966
3. ASTRAL WEEKS (**ASTRAL WEEKS**) - VAN MORRISON 1968
4. THE END (**THE DOORS**) - THE DOORS 1967
5. HEROIN (**THE VELVET UNDERGROUND & NICO**) – THE VELVET UNDERGROUND & NICO 1967
6. A DAY IN THE LIFE (**SGT PEPPER'S LONELY HEARTS CLUB BAND**) - THE BEATLES 1967
7. MIDNIGHT RAMBLER (**LET IT BLEED**) - THE ROLLING STONES 1969
8. VOODOO CHILE (**ELECTRIC LADYLAND**) - THE JIMI HENDRIX EXPERIENCE 1968
9. DOWN BY THE RIVER (**EVERYBODY KNOWS THIS IS NOWHERE**) – NEIL YOUNG 1969
10. ALONE AGAIN OR (**FOREVER CHANGES**) – LOVE 1967
11. THAT'LL BE THE DAY (**THE "CHIRPING" CRICKETS**) – THE CRICKETS 1957
12. I HEARD IT THROUGH THE GRAPEVINE (**I HEARD IT THROUGH THE GRAPEVINE**) – MARVIN GAYE 1968
13. FORTUNATE SON (**WILLY AND THE POOR BOYS**) - CREEDENCE CLEARWATER REVIVAL 1969
14. VISIONS OF JOHANNA (**BLONDE ON BLONDE**) – BOB DYLAN 1966

15 SONG FOR OUR ANCESTORS (**SAILOR**) - STEVE MILLER BAND 1968

16 THE COURT OF THE CRIMSON KING (**IN THE COURT OF THE CRIMSON KING**) - KING CRIMSON 1969

17 DESOLATION ROW (**HIGHWAY 61 REVISITED**) – BOB DYLAN 1965

18 SYMPATHY FOR THE DEVIL (**BEGGARS BANQUET**) – THE ROLLING STONES 1968

19 LUCY IN THE SKY WITH DIAMONDS (**SGT PEPPER'S LONELY HEARTS CLUB BAND**) – THE BEATLES 1967

20 WHITE RABBIT (**SURREALISTIC PILLOW**) - JEFFERSON AIRPLANE 1967

21 YOU REALLY GOT ME (**KINKS**) – THE KINKS 1964

22 KING HARVEST (HAS SURELY COME) (**THE BAND**) - THE BAND 1969

23 WHOLE LOTTA LOVE (**LED ZEPPELIN II**) - LED ZEPPELIN 1969

24 ELEANOR RIGBY (**REVOLVER**) – THE BEATLES 1966

25 PIECE OF MY HEART (**CHEAP THRILLS**) – BIG BROTHER & THE HOLDING COMPANY 1968

26 STUCK INSIDE OF MOBILE WITH THE MEMPHIS BLUES AGAIN (**BLONDE ON BLONDE**) – BOB DYLAN 1966

27 WOULDN'T IT BE NICE (**PET SOUNDS**) – THE BEACH BOYS 1966

28 SUNSHINE OF YOUR LOVE (**DISRAELI GEARS**) – CREAM 1967

29 DEAR PRUDENCE (**THE BEATLES**) – THE BEATLES 1968

30 KICK OUT THE JAMS (**KICK OUT THE JAMS**) - MC5 1969

31	EIGHT MILES HIGH (**FIFTH DIMENSION**) – THE BYRDS 1966
32	COME TOGETHER (**ABBEY ROAD**) – THE BEATLES 1969
33	NORWEGIAN WOOD (THIS BIRD HAS FLOWN) (**RUBBER SOUL**) – THE BEATLES 1965
34	ARE YOU EXPERIENCED? (**ARE YOU EXPERIENCED**) – THE JIMI HENDRIX EXPERIENCE 1967
35	SUBTERRANEAN HOMESICK BLUES (**BRINGING IT ALL BACK HOME**) – BOB DYLAN 1965
36	BLUE TRAIN (**BLUE TRAIN**) – JOHN COLTRANE 1957
37	BROKEN ARROW (**BUFFALO SPRINGFIELD AGAIN**) – BUFFALO SPRINGFIELD 1967
38	HIDEAWAY (**BLUES BREAKERS WITH ERIC CLAPTON**) – JOHN MAYALL 1966
39	ROCK & ROLL MUSIC (**ONE DOZEN BERRYS**) – CHUCK BERRY 1958
40	SIN CITY (**THE GILDED PALACE OF SIN**) – FLYING BURRITO BROTHERS 1969
41	MR TAMBOURINE MAN (**MR TAMBOURINE MAN**) – THE BYRDS 1965
42	CHAIN OF FOOLS (**LADY SOUL**) – ARETHA FRANKLIN 1968
43	MY GENERATION (**THE WHO SINGS MY GENERATION**) – THE WHO 1965
44	GLORIA (**THE ANGRY YOUNG THEM**) – THEM 1965
45	BORN TO BE WILD (**STEPPENWOLF**) – STEPPENWOLF 1968
46	PRESENCE OF THE LORD (**BLIND FAITH**) – BLIND FAITH 1969

47	INTERSTELLAR OVERDRIVE (**THE PIPER AT THE GATES OF DAWN**) – PINK FLOYD 1967
48	DAZED AND CONFUSED (**LED ZEPPELIN**) – LED ZEPPELIN 1969
49	THE SOUND OF SILENCE (**SOUNDS OF SILENCE**) – SIMON & GARFUNKEL 1966
50	HELP! (**HELP!**) – THE BEATLES 1965
51	RIP IT UP (**HERE'S LITTLE RICHARD**) – LITTLE RICHARD 1957
52	TAXMAN (**REVOLVER**) – THE BEATLES 1966
53	PEOPLE GET READY (**PEOPLE GET READY**) – THE IMPRESSIONS 1965
54	CAN'T BUY ME LOVE (**A HARD DAY'S NIGHT**) – THE BEATLES 1964
55	I'M WAITING FOR THE MAN (**THE VELVET UNDERGROUND & NICO**) – THE VELVET UNDERGROUND & NICO 1967
56	YESTERDAY (**HELP!**) – THE BEATLES 1965
57	THE CRYSTAL SHIP (**THE DOORS**) – THE DOORS 1967
58	WAY TO BLUE (**FIVE LEAVES LEFT**) – NICK DRAKE 1969
59	CALIFORNIA DREAMIN' (**IF YOU CAN BELIEVE YOUR EYES AND EARS**) – THE MAMAS & THE PAPAS 1966
60	SPOONFUL (**HOWLIN' WOLF**) – HOWLIN' WOLF 1962
61	CANDY SAYS (**THE VELVET UNDERGROUND**) – THE VELVET UNDERGROUND 1969
62	I'VE BEEN LOVING YOU TOO LONG (**OTIS BLUE**) – OTIS REDDING 1965
63	BLUEJEAN BOP! (**BLUEJEAN BOP!**) – GENE VINCENT 1956

64   WITH A LITTLE HELP FROM MY FRIENDS (**WITH A LITTLE HELP FROM MY FRIENDS**) – JOE COCKER 1969

65   I CAN HEAR MUSIC (**20/20**) – THE BEACH BOYS 1969

66   ...1983 (A MERMAN I SHOULD TURN TO BE) (**ELECTRIC LADYLAND**) - THE JIMI HENDRIX EXPERIENCE 1968

67   ANDMOREAGAIN (**FOREVER CHANGES**) - LOVE 1967

68   FAREWELL, FAREWELL (**LIEGE AND LIEF**) – FAIRPORT CONVENTION 1969

69   GETTING BETTER (**SGT PEPPER'S LONELY HEARTS CLUB BAND**) – THE BEATLES 1967

70   MADAME GEORGE (**ASTRAL WEEKS**) – VAN MORRISON 1968

71   ON THE WAY HOME (**LAST TIME AROUND**) – BUFFALO SPRINGFIELD 1968

72   THE WEAVER'S ANSWER (**FAMILY ENTERTAINMENT**) – FAMILY 1969

73   THE WEIGHT (**MUSIC FROM BIG PINK**) – THE BAND 1968

74   YOU'RE GONNA MISS ME (**THE PSYCHEDELIC SOUNDS OF THE 13TH FLOOR ELEVATORS**) – THE 13TH FLOOR ELEVATORS 1966

75   EVERYDAY PEOPLE (**STAND!**) – SLY & THE FAMILY STONE 1969

76   MARRAKESH EXPRESS (**CROSBY, STILLS & NASH**) – CROSBY, STILLS & NASH 1969

77   CITADEL (**THEIR SATANIC MAJESTIES REQUEST**) – THE ROLLING STONES 1967

78   WHO DO YOU LOVE PART 1 (**HAPPY TRAILS**) – QUICKSILVER MESSENGER SERVICE 1969

79	TURN AROUND (**BRADLEY'S BARN**) – THE BEAU BRUMMELS 1968
80	THE WITCH (**HERE ARE THE SONICS**) – THE SONICS 1965
81	THINGS WE SAID TODAY (**A HARD DAY'S NIGHT**) – THE BEATLES 1964
82	BECK'S BOLERO (**TRUTH**) – JEFF BECK 1968
83	THE LETTER (**THE LETTER/NEON RAINBOW**) – BOX TOPS 1967
84	WHEN THE MUSIC'S OVER (**STRANGE DAYS**) – THE DOORS 1967
85	YESTERDAY'S PAPERS (**BETWEEN THE BUTTONS**) – THE ROLLING STONES 1967
86	VETERAN'S DAY POPPY (**TROUT MASK REPLICA**) - CAPTAIN BEEFHEART & HIS MAGIC BAND 1969
87	IF I WERE A CARPENTER (**TIM HARDIN 2**) - TIM HARDIN 1967
88	SO WHAT (**KIND OF BLUE**) - MILES DAVIS 1959
89	GOOD TIMES BAD TIMES (**LED ZEPPELIN**) – LED ZEPPELIN 1969
90	A SONG FOR JEFFREY (**THIS WAS**) - JETHRO TULL 1968
91	COWGIRL IN THE SAND (**EVERYBODY KNOWS THIS IS NOWHERE**) – NEIL YOUNG 1969
92	RAINBOW CHASER (**ALL OF US**) – NIRVANA 1968
93	ON THE ROAD AGAIN (**BOOGIE WITH CANNED HEAT**) – CANNED HEAT 1968
94	DAYDREAM (**DAYDREAM**) – THE LOVIN' SPOONFUL 1966
95	I'M A LOSER (**BEATLES FOR SALE**) – THE BEATLES 1964
96	GROOVIN' (**GROOVIN'**) – THE YOUNG RASCALS 1967

97	ABSOLUTELY SWEET MARIE (**BLONDE ON BLONDE**) – BOB DYLAN 1966
98	SON OF A PREACHER MAN (**DUSTY IN MEMPHIS**) – DUSTY SPRINGFIELD 1969
99	LAZY SUNDAY (**OGDENS' NUT GONE FLAKE**) – THE SMALL FACES 1968
100	EUROPEAN SON (TO DELMORE SCHWARTZ) (**THE VELVET UNDERGROUND & NICO**) – THE VELVET UNDERGROUND & NICO 1967

(11)

EXILE ON MAIN STREET – THE ROLLING STONES (1972)

(*Rocks Off/Rip This Joint/Shake Your Hips/Casino Boogie/Tumbling Dice/Sweet Virginia/Torn And Frayed/ Sweet Black Angel/Loving Cup/Happy/Turd On The Run/ Ventilator Blues/I Just Want To See His Face/Let It Loose/ All Down The Line/Stop Breaking Down/Shine A Light/ Soul Survivor*)

Top Track: Happy

The Rolling Stones consistently challenged the Beatles during the sixties as the best British band. By 1967 they were losing the battle, distracted by disastrous dabbling with psychedelic concepts, so it came as a relief when, in 1968, they discarded the hippy robes and resumed their bluesy brand of rock. To hear them playing *Jumping Jack Flash* rather than *Sing This All Together* was one of the purifying, salvation moments in rock's still youthful life. From that point onwards they enjoyed a renewed burst of energy, releasing several first-class albums.

In 1971, in the wake of the demise of their main British rivals, the highly-refined **Sticky Fingers** strengthened popular opinion that they were the greatest rock 'n' roll band on earth. Any lingering doubts concerning their credentials were firmly banished with the release of **Exile On Main Street**. As with any four-sider, questions were raised regarding the inclusion of certain tunes but ultimately, it was the sprawling musical range that made it so captivating.

Sales were assisted by allowing a few songs to be made available on a floppy vinyl, given away free with the New Musical Express. The freebie didn't contain the entire tracks, only edited snippets tantalisingly sufficient to enthuse curious interest. The key songs featured were *All Down The Line*, *Happy*, *Tumbling Dice* and *Shine A Light*. It was clever use of the more accessible styles found on the LP. The same couldn't be said for the photography adorning the album's cover, displaying unattractive mug shots featuring misfits from society's gutter.

Sounding at times as though conceived in a subterranean setting, **Exile On Main Street** is often viewed as rock's greatest basement album. There was one simple explanation for this, namely that in the most part it was recorded using a mobile unit outside Keith Richards' home in Villefranche, France. Undoubtedly, the unconventional surroundings contributed to the relatively unsophisticated feel, certainly in comparison with the slick production personified by its predecessor.

The band's fascination with America continued unabated, flourishing in an environment textured by the Blues (*Stop Breaking Down*), Gospel (*Shine A Light*) and Country (*Sweet Virginia*). Although not getting any younger, they held no wish for the quiet life, with their tough, hard-image thumping through on *Turd On The Run*, *Rip This Joint* and *Rocks Off*. The extra vinyl permitted them an experimental license, absorbing musical influences to produce a stunningly expansive set. The downhill slide from glory began not long afterwards.

(12)

THE VELVET UNDERGROUND & NICO (1967)

(Sunday Morning/I'm Waiting For The Man/Femme Fatale/Venus In Furs/Run, Run, Run/All Tomorrow's Parties/Heroin/There She Goes Again/I'll Be Your Mirror/The Black Angel's Death Song/European Son (To Delmore Schwartz))

Top Track: Heroin

In a few days during spring 1966 Lou Reed, John Cale, Sterling Morrison, Maureen Tucker and Nico recorded the basic composition to a sound that has influenced rock musicians ever since. Folklore recalls that those who heard these songs were so inspired by their downtrodden imagery they were compelled to form a band. Not true, of course, but **The Velvet Underground & Nico** (released in March 1967) hints at being performed by artists living in a compressed environment, with a sufficiently simplistic approach to suggest anyone could replicate the style.

Sunday Morning belonged in a land of lullabies and sunny summer skies, but on closer observation of the lyrics it became apparent that something was wrong. Reed's subdued words added an earthly balance to delightful musical arrangements. From this point onwards, it was all downhill for normality as track after track focused on sinister, back-street and dark alley, nomadic existence. References to drugs *I'm Waiting For The Man*, *Run Run Run*, *Heroin* and sexual deviation *Venus In Furs*, were littered like street debris. The really strange thing was that the softer tunes, *I'll Be Your Mirror*, *Femme Fatale* and *All Tomorrow's Parties*, intermingled harmoniously with the hard-edged controversial selections, culminating in the frantic thrash finale, *European Son (To Delmore Schwartz)*.

Even during 1967, when drugs were no longer a lifestyle choice reserved for hippies, the debut by the VU was still too dangerous for mass consumption. The inquisitive that heard it were simultaneously shocked and excited by rock's newfound capabilities, mesmerised by entrancing riffs and lyrical waywardness. Lovers of stripped back to basics, adrenalin-fused rock are highly recommended to check this out.

(13)

THE BEATLES (1968)

(Back In The USSR/Dear Prudence/Glass Onion/Ob-La-Di, Ob-La-Da/Wild Honey Pie/The Continuing Story Of Bungalow Bill/While My Guitar Gently Weeps/Happiness Is A Warm Gun/Martha My Dear/I'm So Tired/ Blackbird/ Piggies/Rocky Raccoon/Don't Pass Me By/Why Don't We Do It In The Road?/I Will/Julia/Birthday/Yer Blues/ Mother Nature's Son/Everybody's Got Something To Hide Except Me And My Monkey/Sexy Sadie/Helter Skelter/ Long, Long, Long/Revolution 1/Honey Pie/Savoy Truffle/ Cry Baby Cry/Revolution 9/Good Night)

Top Track: Dear Prudence

Unlike **Sgt Pepper's Lonely Hearts Club Band** with its colourful sleeve portraying celebrities, **The Beatles** came packaged in a plain white cover, front and back – imaginatively dubbed The White Album. In common with the predecessor, however, there were freebies. Not picture card cut-outs, but straightforward photos of the real Beatles. Yes John, Paul, George and Ringo were back, rather than the fictitious group wearing peculiar costumes. They were returning to their old selves (or were they?), only now with much longer hair. As before, a lyric sheet was provided so that the freshly bought LP just needed to be placed on the turntable, and with words to hand the fan could join in.

A double LP afforded scope to assert their individual identities, theoretically liberating them to satisfy aspirations. Lennon was keen to pursue Avant-Garde innovation in conjunction with Yoko Ono, the presence of whom added to tensions within the band. So strong was his self-belief that it begged an answer as to whether he had taken leave of his senses. *Revolution No 9*, for over eight minutes, meandered through a collage of weird sounds, backward winding tapes and inconsequential film soundtrack clips. It stretched the definition of what constituted 'music', offering aural pleasure to virtually no one. Redemption for Lennon, nonetheless, could be found through an enviable ability to pen memorable tunes (*Glass Onion, Sexy Sadie* and *Cry Baby Cry* spring to mind).

Meanwhile, the continued growth in Harrison's song-writing was self-evident, notably on *While My Guitar Gently Weeps* featuring guest guitarist Eric Clapton, and the poignant *Long, Long, Long*. Although a suspect writer, democracy reached new limits with Ringo providing the lack lustre *Don't Pass Me By*. McCartney, as always, maintained pop normality, with *Back In The USSR, Mother Nature's Son* and *Blackbird* typifying effortless class.

The Beatles had many wide-ranging, lasting qualities (*Happiness Is A Warm Gun/Dear Prudence/Helter Skelter* for starters). From the pumped-up rock of *Birthday*, through to mellow Folk (*Julia* and *I Will*) and pop bliss with the quaint *Ob-La-Di, Ob-La-Da* and *The Continuing Story Of Bungalow Bill*, there was a tune for everyone. However, the freedom to be indulgent was gained at a price. It's an often stated opinion by critics and record buyers, that reducing the track count by half could possibly have made this the greatest album of all-time. Such an ultimate accolade would be denied due to so many underperforming songs. Enigmatically, even allowing for the incomprehensible inclusions, it represents an historic document, a watershed when the cracks in the Beatles machine became irreparable.

(14)

BLOOD ON THE TRACKS – BOB DYLAN (1975)

(*Tangled Up In Blue/Simple Twist Of Fate/You're A Big Girl Now/Idiot Wind/You're Gonna Make Me Lonesome When You Go/Meet Me In The Morning/Lily, Rosemary & The Jack Of Hearts/If You See Her, Say Hello/Shelter From The Storm/ Buckets Of Rain*)

Top Track: Tangled Up In Blue

At the time of writing his 15th studio album Dylan was in the throes of marital breakdown. This period in his life resulted in anxious thoughts, many revealed via confessional songs on the aptly titled **Blood On The Tracks**. Perhaps due to necessity to seek comfort through familiarity, his return to musical form coincided with a re-discovery of his Folk heritage.

On *Tangled Up In Blue* he gazed backwards for solutions to a crisis, whilst simultaneously acknowledging that the world had moved on and old friends were no longer around. It painted a depressingly familiar picture for divorced couples finding themselves on their own, suddenly realising just how alone they were. Where were their friends from the happy, good old days?

It was this lyrical empathy with challenging traumas that gave this album life-affirming strength. With his life in disarray, a sense of desperation and confusion prevailed, pitifully on *If You See Her, Say Hello*, whilst resignation to troubled circumstances dominated the bizarrely up-tempo *You're Gonna Make Me Lonesome When You Go*. With **Blood On The Tracks** Dylan kissed goodbye to past failures and yet reached out to former glories, these ten tracks hallmarked by the influence of his acoustic peaks from the previous decade.

To a considerable degree, he was perplexed by the popular reception given to the LP. How could it be that his emotional pain meant so much and to so many? Clearly, his return to narrative tales, mainly drawn from first-hand experiences, struck home with those enduring similar turmoil. The concurring themes running throughout reflected at length over failed relationships, collapsing personal commitments, whilst all along a significant undercurrent made a harrowing presence. The sixties generation had grown a little older, a little wiser, with a deepened realisation that they couldn't change the world.

(15)

BORN IN THE U.S.A. – BRUCE SPRINGSTEEN (1984)

(*Born In The U.S.A./Cover Me/Darlington County/Working On The Highway/Downbound Train/I'm On Fire/No Surrender/Bobby Jean/I'm Goin' Down/Glory Days/ Dancing In The Dark/My Hometown*)

Top Track: Downbound Train

After the courageous (or commercially suicidal) decision to release the downbeat, Folk-orientated **Nebraska** two years earlier, The Boss returned in 1984 brimming with high-octane, arena-pleasers. Wrongly translated by politicians as a rallying cry upholding virtuous American society, the new album's title-track stood for anything but. In all honesty, there was little ambiguity in Springsteen's message, the lyrics emphatically hitting home some harsh truths. Emphasis was also placed on that most sensitive episode in contemporary US history, Vietnam. With venom, a generation's anger exploded with revulsion at the wrong-doings committed in a foreign country. Rarely had US rock been so highly-charged, delivered with such conviction.

Springsteen's depressed assessment of life in modern America continued on *Cover Me*. It was musically fast-driven but behind the facade there existed entrenched pessimism. *Working On The Highway*, meanwhile, was a knees-up, full-throttle party-shaker, but again defeatist despair reared its head. The highpoint was the start to Side Two (vinyl/cassette), *No Surrender* – a roaring celebration of youthful optimism, with a proud proclamation that more could be learned from short pop songs than in school. It was a readily understood statement by the 45s generation. Such triumph didn't last long, as even on Springsteen's finest rocker, a dejected philosophy had the final say.

Born In The U.S.A. looked through the microscope, viewing perspectives on life as seen by the underdog (the unemployed, the Vietnam Veteran, repressed souls). Even the staunchly loyal fans from his early career could rejoice at his acute lyrical observations. LYRICS ENCLOSED the front cover boasted. It was a justifiable decision, ensuring no misunderstandings – these were not songs upholding pure wholesome values, nor were they a patriotic songbook for modern U.S.A.

Singles were culled with alarming regularity (no fewer than seven), with the rousing dance/rock anthem *Dancing In The Dark* almost giving him a US Number 1. Another apt title for the album would have been the Best of Bruce Springsteen, with every track exemplifying articulated artistry – there simply weren't any dull moments. As for the LP cover featuring a close-up of Springsteen's butt? Some observers assumed there had to be a meaningful reason. This, however, was The Boss, the modern poet and as always an explanation lay in down-to-earth pragmatism. Several pictures were considered but the general consensus was the one of his ass looked better than his face! And so that was that, a truthful answer for an honest record bursting with integrity.

(16)
ABBEY ROAD - THE BEATLES (1969)

(*Come Together/Something/Maxwell's Silver Hammer/Oh! Darling/Octopus's Garden/I Want You (She's So Heavy)/ Here Comes The Sun/Because/You Never Give Me Your Money/Sun King/Mean Mr Mustard/Polythene Pam/She Came In Through The Bathroom Window/Golden Slumbers/Carry That Weight/The End/Her Majesty*)

Top Track: Come Together

In September 1969 the Beatles released what, in the end, was their last new LP (although released in May 1970, the sessions for **Let It Be** pre-dated **Abbey Road** back to the early months of '69). The much-mimicked LP cover featured a photograph of the band walking across a zebra crossing. It seemed an innocuous picture but rumours began circulating that within it were symbolic meanings leading to one conclusion - Paul McCartney was dead!

The evidence could be deciphered by unscrambling numerous clues. McCartney was bare-footed (the others wore shoes), Lennon was dressed in white (representing a priest), Harrison was wearing a denim jacket (a grave-digger) and Ringo wore black (the undertaker). McCartney walked out of step with the other three and was the only Beatle smoking. Then there was the car parked next to the kerb, of course a VW Beetle, but take a look at the registration number, 28IF, signifying his age at next birthday. The elaborate hoax, merely the latest in a long line of Paul Is Dead theories, unhelpfully distracted from the real story. The Beatles had a new album, acclaimed as their best by several critics.

The appearance of Linda Eastman and Yoko Ono fuelled pre-existing frictions within the group, the impressionable shadow of the latter hovering strongly over Lennon's shoulders. The music, nevertheless, showed that although there was inter-feuding, they were still able to cut fine tunes. Lennon kept matters serious, bookending Side 1 with *Come Together* and the chilled-rock epic *I Want You (She's So Heavy)*. In between, Harrison contributed his first single, *Something*, McCartney doodled with hysterical storylines, *Maxwell's Silver Hammer* and *Oh! Darling*, and Ringo gave his usual best effort, *Octopus's Garden*.

However, it was Side 2 where the action lay. *Here Comes The Sun* offered further evidence that the Quiet One was fast transforming in to a song-writing force to be reckoned with – the greatest Beatles song not released as a 45? *Because* showcased their superb harmonies and up next, the famed medley that harnessed an array of musical styles. Although the tracks had minimal lyrical relevance to each other, when sequenced they duly became integral components of something much larger. Who were *Mean Mr Mustard* and *Polythene Pam* and what did it matter? Some songs were barely a minute long coming across as half-completed sketches, but woven together they produced a surreal beauty.

They finished with sad news (*The End*). It was in keeping with the album's character, concise and precise. It was the end, in all but name. The foregone conclusion would be delayed until early 1970 but the Beatles were effectively no longer a band.

(17)

GRIEVOUS ANGEL – GRAM PARSONS (1974)

(*Return Of The Grievous Angel/Hearts On Fire/I Can't Dance/Brass Buttons/$1000 Wedding/Cash On The Barrelhead/Hickory Wind/Love Hurts/Ooh Las Vegas/In My Hour Of Darkness*)
Top Track: *Return Of The Grievous Angel*

Parsons' pioneering work with the International Submarine Band and the Byrds laid the foundation stones. It was, however, with the Flying Burrito Brothers and their 1969 highpoint, ***The Gilded Palace Of Sin***, that his fusion of soft-edged rock, with a contemporary Country sound yearning for change from its traditional boundaries, reached early perfection. Failure to capitalise on widespread critical acclaim, coupled with general disillusionment, resulted in his decision to venture out on a solo adventure. Exacerbated by alcohol and drug abuse, initial recording sessions were unproductive, failing to match the quality attained during the sixties.

It wasn't until late '72 that anything worthy of consideration alongside his previous work materialised, culminating in the release of his fledgling solo LP. ***GP*** emphasised an aim to stretch mainstream Country's limits, and in vocal companion, Emmylou Harris, he found a stabilising balance for his gritted sentiments. *Still Feeling Blue*, *A Song For You*, *She* and *Big Mouth Blues* characterised breathtaking ambition, a man on a mission. It was an album overflowing with bluegrass heritage, but Parsons had better ideas on the direction that banjos, fiddles and pedal steel guitars should go.

Grievous Angel lays down the benchmark by which Country albums will always be measured. Again, Harris was the invaluable mother-earth guardian angel steadying depressed tales of disappearing hope and dejected romance. His best can be found here, *Love Hurts*, *Hearts On Fire*, *In My Hour Of Darkness* and especially, *Return Of The Grievous Angel*. The latter ticker-taped a litany of references to Southern States lifestyle, past and present (a good saloon, Bible belt, billboards and truckstops). The musical arrangement replicated this sense of journey, a feeling of self-fulfilling destiny – imagine being saddled-up on a horse, riding off in to the sunset and you'll get the idea - the best song for the road ever?

The album's origins make it surprising that the completed work should be so rich, a woven tapestry of rock and Country, old and new. During its making in 1973 Parsons had few fresh compositions available and, although hastily preparing *In My Hour Of Darkness* and *Return Of The Grievous Angel*, there remained a strong reliance on previously rejected material, together with various Country standards. With assistance from Harris and support from Elvis Presley's Hot Band, a haphazard selection of songs were sculptured to form pristine beauty - debate will, however, forever rage about whether the final listings on the LP were true to his intentions.

With inspired input from former eras, *$1000 Wedding*, *Brass Buttons*, *Ooh Las Vegas* and the live medley *Cash On The Barrelhead/Hickory Wind*, a strong consensus emerged that God's Own Singer had devised the ultimate Cosmic American Music. Sadly, rather than the start of an artistic surge that would see him champion Country rock, he died from an overdose in September 1973. Posthumously released, **Grievous Angel** begs the question – if only.

(18)
PSYCHOCANDY – THE JESUS AND MARY CHAIN (1985)

(Just Like Honey/The Living End/Taste The Floor/The Hardest Walk/Cut Dead/In A Hole/Taste Of Cindy/Some Candy Talking/Never Understand/Inside Me/Sowing Seeds/My Little Underground/You Trip Me Up/ Something's Wrong/It's So Hard)

Top Track: You Trip Me Up

Their debut was one of the most seminal and divisive releases during the eighties, splitting critical opinion in a way not seen since the Sex Pistols. The recordings were outrageously distorted, with track after track suggesting the dials on the amps were turned well into the red zone. Where had this music been assembled – in a derelict basement or deep underground in a decaying torture chamber (*Never Understand* makes you wonder whether someone was receiving the thumbscrew treatment)? Also, were the musicians, especially the lead singer, even in the same room as the recording equipment? **Psychocandy** threw out the text book on how music should sound, heroically going against the grain. It was a gamble that paid off, maybe not commercially, but unarguably in terms of lasting credibility.

Founding members, William and Jim Reid, originated from East Kilbride but for thought-starters looked westwards and backwards to Punk, the Velvet Underground, the Beach Boys and Phil Spector's Wall of Sound. Underneath the demented, aural carnage that terrorised these fifteen songs existed some of the prettiest tunes ever committed to disc, battling for prominence against chaotic guitar feedback.

The intro beats to *Just Like Honey* were copied from *Be My Baby* but such co-ordinated respect was far from typical. Psychotic drumbeats and menacing, 'intrusive' feedback were more the preferred method of construction, making for an enlivened experience. 1:12 minutes into *Taste The Floor* and the immediacy of *In A Hole* sounded like a dentist's drill plugged into an amplifier, immortalising electric chords suffering at the hands of a savage attack. *The Living End, Inside Me, My Little Underground* and *You Trip Me Up* let sparks fly in all directions, unadulterated craziness. 10/15 tracks clocked in at less than 3:00 minutes (*Taste Of Cindy* a mere 1:42), indicating a band with an urgent agenda. Alas, few were paying attention at the time.

During the sunrise years of Compact Disc, albums were meant to accurately reflect highly-polished production, with every instrument heard as though in the recording studio. The Chain had other ideas. Everything was far out of place, the arrangements appeared disjointed, seemingly not quite finished, but there lay the beauty. Lovers of slickness scorn at the apparent disregard for crystal clear purity, whereas the open-minded treasure the precarious courage to push feedback beyond 'sensible' usage. If anything, CD enhances that schizophrenic jaunt through 25 years of flashbacks condensed into 39 minutes. Hindsight shows that from 1980-85 few British records have made a permanent impact - **Psychocandy** is one of them.

(19)
WHATEVER PEOPLE SAY I AM, THAT'S WHAT I'M NOT – ARCTIC MONKEYS (2006)

(The View From The Afternoon/I Bet You Look Good On The Dancefloor/Fake Tales Of San Francisco/Dancing Shoes/You Probably Couldn't See For The Lights But You Were Staring Straight At Me/Still Take You Home/Riot Van/Red Light Indicates Doors Are Secured/Mardy Bum/ Perhaps Vampires Is A Bit Strong But.../When The Sun Goes Down/From The Ritz To The Rubble/A Certain Romance)

Top Track: *I Bet You Look Good On The Dancefloor*

Testament that rock's yesteryears still influenced the contemporary UK scene was found during January 2006. Paradoxically, Arctic Monkeys also achieved fame thanks to a cult-following that used innovation, notably Myspace, to get the word of mouth recommendation out. With lightning speed they attained a supersonic rise from unknown Yorkshire act to Britain's hottest property. Where other tipped bands before stumbled when it came to the critical point of deliverance, Sheffield's new heroes effortlessly satisfied the high promise. Not since the Strokes had a debut justified the hype and, from a British perspective, a long 12 years had passed since **Definitely Maybe**.

Linked to the same lyrical family tree as Ray Davies, Paul Weller and Pete Doherty, Alex Turner's observations on 21st Century urban lifestyle in the UK were painfully recognisable. Fraught with stressed stories of police brutality, drunken binges and late-night brawls, the band's debut ominously exposed modern youth culture in all its infamous glory. Enthusiasm by critics was almost unanimous, some suggesting that they were as good as Oasis, others noted similarities with the Clash, a few drew just short of ridiculous comparison with the ultimate British band from the sixties. To grey-haired rock fans it seemed incredulous that music played so frantic, spewing lyrics derived from gutter experiences and self-indulgent excess, could be viewed as essential listening. To anyone younger than 30, or perhaps 20, here were songs that mirrored life.

This band had plenty to discuss and, with thoughtful intellect unbecoming at such a young age, they pinpointed a Britain convulsing in a manic frenzy, an ethos born from no time for idle talk. In essence, these were teenage characteristics, a message intended for them, but misunderstood by 'mature' listeners failing to spot the luminous signposts that indicated some obvious influences. Those inspirations were taken mainly from Punk's rotten core, levelled by a street-corner mentality absorbing hoodies, cigarette stubs and alcoholic stench.

I Bet You Look Good On The Dancefloor and *When The Sun Goes Down* led the initial charge, both topping the UK charts. It was nothing short of an astonishing achievement given their absence of commercial appeal, notably the latter's prostitution theme. Further stand-out tracks included *The View From The Afternoon*, *Fake Tales Of San Francisco*, *Mardy Bum* and the anthemic *A Certain Romance* – all fanning an instant mystique surrounding the interview-shy lads.

Whatever People Say I Am, That's What I'm Not broke UK sales records, becoming the fastest selling debut in its first week. Presumably, it was purchased by eagerly appreciative kids and bemused 'still got the finger on the rock pulse' Dads, sucked in by rave reviews and unprecedented hype. Radiohead's initial presence at the top end of all-time greatest albums charts was hard to stomach for some music scholars. To find suddenly, literally suddenly, Arctic Monkeys also heralded amongst rock's cream was surely too much, far too soon, but only time will tell. For now at least, their debut defines a generation, in much the same way as the equivalents by Oasis, the Stone Roses and Sex Pistols had done.

(20)
THE BENDS – RADIOHEAD (1995)

(Planet Telex/The Bends/High & Dry/Fake Plastic Trees/Bones/(Nice Dream)/Just/My Iron Lung/Bullet Proof... I Wish I Was/Black Star/Sulk/Street Spirit (Fade Out))

Top Track: *Street Spirit (Fade Out)*

They achieved minimal success with **Pablo Honey** (1993), the key track *Creep* gaining popular support in the unlikely hearts of prisoners on Death Row. The lyrics hit home in the minds of Uncle Sam's poisoned souls, taking on albatross proportion – Radiohead, the band who recorded 'that song'! Two versions existed, the best being the album's, featuring a swear word that added an angry texture to an already highly-charged potion. For radio/TV broadcast the F-word needed removing to appease consumer sensitive programmers. Somehow, its replacement lost the ferocious cutting edge, the alteration of just one word resulting in the absence of street-wise aggression.

The Bends signified a more discerning ideology, instigating a giant leap from relative obscurity beyond a hardcore fan base, into the minds of the intellectual elite. Breakages were uppermost in the band's thoughts, specifically on *Planet Telex*, *Fake Plastic Trees* and *High & Dry*, all of which suitably inscribed emotional meltdown. Cheerful days were long gone but the electric guitar was given a celebratory resurrection, with sky-high solos gracing *High & Dry* and *(Nice Dream)*. Highpoints were plentiful, if not in lyrical optimism, at least with musical generosity. *Bones* (complete with manic feedback) , together with the title-track, restored conventional rock chords, whilst *(Nice Dream)* resorted to lesson one guitar licks backed by Bowie circa '71 harmonies. Angst of a mature kind provided the signature to *My Iron Lung*, with a probing verdict reached on faith.

It was building towards something spectacular, suggesting an impending storm. *Bullet Proof... I Wish I Was* slowed the tempo, *Black Star* speeded things up, *Sulk* brooded and then, a song to justify Britain's standing in the world. *Street Spirit (Fade Out)* – it was so simple, derived around a few repetitive chords and courted by a stream of harrowing anecdotes troubled by depressive visions. It sounded incredibly fundamental, as if anyone could have recorded it – a crucial quality that forms part of the constitution to any exceptional art-form.

The band's dramatic promotion to rock's top flight was aided by sophisticated videos accompanying the singles. Whilst many groups opted for eye-catching visuals using sexy women and fast cars as a focal-point, this superficial perspective wouldn't work in the world of cold, dark lunar landscapes occupied by Radiohead. The video for *Street Spirit (Fade Out)* kept the watcher intrigued, as normal motion continuously slowed down to almost a virtual stop, only to speed up and so forth. Gravity-defying sequences, filmed in black and white, both mystified and charmed. The true strength, however, was Thom Yorke's stark musing over pressurised uncertainties, with lyrical descriptions readily recognisable to anyone living in the late 20th Century.

Radiohead didn't belong in the surrealistic dream shared by hippies. Although there were occasional skirmishes with rock's golden days, **The Bends** was possessed by quintessential pre-millennium anxieties. It rightly received 'classic' status, an accolade that grows as the years pass.

(21)
ELECTRIC LADYLAND – THE JIMI HENDRIX EXPERIENCE (1968)

(...And The Gods Made Love/Have You Ever Been (To Electric Ladyland)/Crosstown Traffic/Voodoo Chile/Little Miss Strange/Long Hot Summer Night/Come On (Let The Good Times Roll)/Gypsy Eyes/Burning Of The Midnight Lamp/Rainy Day, Dream Away/1983... (A Merman I Should Turn To Be)/Moon, Turn The Tides...Gently Gently Away/ Still Raining, Still Dreaming/House Burning Down/All Along The Watchtower/Voodoo Chile (Slight Return))

Top Track: *Voodoo Chile*

In 1966 former bass guitarist with the Animals/aspiring band manager, Chas Chandler, said to a relatively unknown, gifted musician from America, that bringing his innovative skills to England would be a beneficial career move. Pursuing this suggestion, and in partnership with two Englishmen, Noel Redding and Mitch Mitchell, the Jimi Hendrix Experience were formed, with Chandler's promise soon paying substantial dividends. *Hey Joe* was an immediate success, with further 45s following, the best being *Purple Haze* and *Manic Depression*. It was, however, through the explorative and improvisational nature of his first two albums, **Are You Experienced?** and **Axis: Bold As Love** that Hendrix stood out.

On reflection, the most startling aspect about his debut LP (and further proof that the professional critic's opinion is not always reliable), was the scale of negative reviews received in the press. Whilst Hendrix's guitar-playing abilities weren't questioned, his intended direction for taking the instrument was met with unease, with some believing that his performance trespassed over to unnecessary forcefulness. Again with hindsight, it's apparent given that contemporary music had hitherto been dominated by pop, **Are You Experienced?** was a major milestone in rock's development. Prior to this LP there was pop, by record's end rock's universe had emphatically begun.

Electric Ladyland was the first album where he gained production control over his recordings; it would also be the last time. It began at a frantic pace with three tracks, *...And The Gods Made Love, Have You Ever Been (To Electric Ladyland)* and *Crosstown Traffic*, speeding by in under six minutes. However, Hendrix's aspiration to progress beyond the confines of conventional rock achieved fruition through the lengthier cuts. With the opening, short-burst, proceedings dealt with, it was down to the serious business.

The elongated *Voodoo Chile*, featuring guest appearances from Steve Winwood (electric organ) and on bass Jack Cassady (from Jefferson Airplane), for fifteen glorious minutes allowed the audience to 'drop in' on what felt like work in progress. There were further gems, the reprise of *Voodoo Chile* and another extended composition, *1983... (A Merman I Should Turn To Be)*. The latter spanned almost the entire Side 3, never waning for a second, as Hendrix's fondness for screeching guitars and the fade in/out technique went into incredulous overdrive. Lest we forget finally, this album also contained an electrified cover of Dylan's *All Along The Watchtower*. **Electric Ladyland** was the closest he came to capturing 'that sound' in his head, channelling it in to music, exactly as he wanted.

(22)

BRYTER LAYTER – NICK DRAKE (1970)

(Introduction/Hazey Jane II/At The Chime Of A City Clock/One Of These Things First/Hazey Jane I/Bryter Layter/Fly/Poor Boy/ Northern Sky/Sunday)

Top Track: At The Chime Of A City Clock

Although blessed by several commercialised Folk songs, Drake's debut, **Five Leaves Left**, failed to register interest other than amongst the cognoscenti. With persuasion from close friends he persevered, the resultant follow-up, **Bryter Layter**, proving to be a far more upbeat, cheerful affair (at least musically). The lyrics, however, gave alarming warnings that this shy man was far from happy.

It began with the first of three instrumentals, the moody, film-score styled, *Introduction*. All three were indescribably quaint but distinctly lacked the strongest characteristic that defined Drake's music, his voice. There was an old-worldly Englishness about his vocals, delicate and with more than a trace of a refined, well-groomed upbringing. Indeed, with a public school education and a financially secure background, he should have been a man with few worries. Yet somehow, his personal life was blighted by self-doubts and episodes of depression.

On *At The Chime Of A City Clock* his lyrics gave cause for concern that life was on a troubling downer for the ill-fated singer/songwriter. On *Poor Boy* (listen here for a supreme example of the saxophone's seductiveness), there were further indications of a nervous character. How could it be that a man handed good fortune became this, depressed and fearing the world in which he lived? That his life ended tragically four years later, inevitably resulted in gravediggers sifting through his lyrics, searching for explanatory clues for his untimely demise. *Northern Sky* succinctly showed desperate thoughts, perceivably pointing apocalyptically to an ominous future.

His big problem was an inability to coherently perform music live, with rare stage appearances usually marred by trembling and inaudible mumbling. Deterred, he shunned the spotlight, a decision that hindered still further his public profile. Drake's graceful music went unnoticed with even the music press devoting little more than a few lines in reviewing his work. That **Bryter Layter** was largely ignored in 1970 remains one of the biggest injustices in music history, making you wonder what might have been. The inquisitive should check this out, for *Hazey Jane II*, *Northern Sky*, *One Of These Things First*, *Poor Boy* and, above all, *At The Chime Of A City Clock* are masterful in their mournful perfection.

(23)

SCREAMADELICA – PRIMAL SCREAM (1991)

(Movin' On Up/Slip Inside This House/Don't Fight It, Feel It/Higher Than The Sun/Inner Flight/Come Together/ Loaded/Damaged/I'm Comin' Down/Higher Than The Sun (A Dub Symphony In Two Parts)/Shine Like Stars)

Top Track: Loaded

The commercial success of experimental trip-hoppers Massive Attack paved the way for others, but the finest exponents of fusing dance, rock, folk, gospel, dub and blues, influenced by a drugs culture were Primal Scream. Early indications that they were formulising something unique were heard on the single, *Loaded*. Complete with an ultra-cool video rekindling the easy-riding biker spirit, the opening narrative words too were the essence of chill. Taking the lately unfashionable electric guitar and adding it to a boiling pot of dance rhythms, *Loaded* was a sign that music in the early-nineties was undergoing a long overdue revamp.

The opening cut on **Screamadelica**, *Movin' On Up*, embraced Gospel spiritualism blended with the slick attitude of the Rolling Stones at their best. It gave the album a flying start, aided by Jimmy Miller's production mastery at the deck, to create a swaggering, cocksure confidence that positively gleamed. The band's primary inspiration, however, originated not from above but a more earthly, traditional source of rock 'n' roll guidance. Hallucinogenic substances were in use during the recording sessions, explaining much of the screwed-up, schizophrenic and anarchic nature of the final product.

The cosmic-floating happiness of drug-manifested highness was evident on the spaced-out *Higher Than The Sun*. *Don't Fight It, Feel It* conveyed several ecstatic dance-floor seminal statements from the era, pounded by a pulsating beat synonymous with the early-nineties drug/house culture. Elsewhere, diversity prospered with sitars on *Slip Inside This House*, Chinese atmospherics on *I'm Comin' Down* through to the dubbed version of *Higher Than The Sun* (billed as a dub symphony in two parts).

At the end of 1995 the influential Select magazine conducted a survey to determine the best albums of the nineties so far. At Number 1, above more predictable choices, was **Screamadelica**.

(24)

THE DOORS (1967)

*(**Break On Through (To The Other Side)/Soul Kitchen/The Crystal Ship/Twentieth Century Fox/Alabama Song (Whisky Bar)/Light My Fire/Back Door Man/I Looked At You/End Of The Night/Take It As It Comes/The End**)*

Top Track: The End

Throughout 1966 the fledgling underground scene in San Francisco continued its ambitious journey, assisted by chemical stimulation. The quality of many bands was too commercial to remain part of a subterranean lifestyle, resulting in the hippy culture sprawling upwards towards the mainstream. The most successful West Coast group, the Doors, scored a massive hit with the edited version of *Light My Fire* topping the US charts during the summer of 1967. It was a gigantic milestone, evidence that the underground had won over the hearts and minds of ordinary record buyers. Now everyone was 'tuning in' and 'dropping out'.

Light My Fire, smouldering with suggestive lyrics, was a pop-orientated tune but even this, at face value, innocent song ran in to trouble with the censors. Surprisingly, it wasn't so much the lyrics laced with sex causing offence but the connection with drugs inferred by the word 'higher'. Ultimately its fabulous hooks, together with glorious electric keyboard punctuations, were too strong to be denied ascendancy up the US charts, least of all by a harmless word. The album version was even better, doubling the track's length and allowing for enchanting, improvisational solos.

There was more to the Doors than straightforward Pop. An examination of their self-titled debut LP revealed a dark side (*Alabama Song*), a care-free philosophy towards drugs (*Break On Through*), romantic poetic beauty (*The Crystal Ship*) and sexual perversion gone completely mad (*The End*). Break On Through contained that dreaded word that so easily upset the public broadcasters. 'High' was repeated several times on the unedited version but on radio/TV the H word mysteriously disappeared, replaced by a conspicuous bleep, the presence of which only brought attention to the missing 'offensive' lyric. Jim Morrison roared his way through the song, in a come and join me if you're brave enough taunt. There were times when his conviction made such a proposition enticing.

The End was an eleven minutes monster that began innocuously with Morrison declaring it was the end (but of what?). Negative lyrical streams ensued, linked by celebrative optimism derived from unrestrained ambition. As the song progressed, it became apparent that he was adopting the persona of Greek mythological character, Oedipus. Changing vocal style from singer to narrator, Morrison walked down the hall, visited his brother's room before resuming to his parents' bedroom. In a psychotic manner he announced his intention to kill his father. Next, his desires for his mother, followed by an unleashed scream. We all knew that the scream obscured a hideous truth.

Morrison typified the new breed in popular music, determined to push his limits of physical and emotional endurance, in a quest for the ultimate exhilaration. His extraordinary lyrics reached out to a wide-ranging audience, in the process acting as a catalyst to the burning fires of the West Coast underground. By the Summer of Love the movement had risen upwards, prompting the celebrated funeral for the mock death of the hippy.

(25)

THE BAND (1969)

(*Across The Great Divide/Rag Mama Rag/The Night They Drove Old Dixie Down/When You Awake/Up On Cripple Creek/Whispering Pines/Jemima Surrender/Rockin' Chair/ Look Out Cleveland/Jawbone/The Unfaithful Servant/King Harvest (Has Surely Come)*))

Top Track: *King Harvest (Has Surely Come)*

For several years Levon Helm (drums), Garth Hudson (organ), Rick Danko (bass guitar), Richard Manuel (piano) and JR (Robbie) Robertson (lead guitar) paid their dues under various guises, most famously as Bob Dylan's backing band. In 1968 they emerged from behind his shadow to release a stunning debut, **Music From Big Pink**. Critical acclaim was lavishly bestowed with stand-out cuts *This Wheel's On Fire*, *The Weight* and *Tears Of Rage* receiving particular acknowledgement. It was a superb record but their self-titled follow-up was even better.

Its rusty-coloured LP cover depicted the five unshaven band members with not a smile to be seen, complementing acutely the tense seriousness of the music within. **The Band** finds Robertson calling the shots, for it was he that provided lyrical input and, although the production was a collective effort, he made the biggest contribution. The songs revived lifestyles from Colonial America, digging deep into the richness of the country's 'ancient' heritage, with an emphasis on people and places. An outstanding example of this was *The Night They Drove Old Dixie Down*, with profound insight in to the battered and bruised thoughts of a soldier during the closing stages of the Civil War. Sharing his story with those who listen, his bleak outlook for the future never fails to induce a poignant response. History brought to life and tearfully channelled into contemporary song.

On *Rockin' Chair* the pipe-puffing, slippers-by-the-fireside mood perfectly captured the contemplativeness of an old-timer. Equally, *Across The Great Divide*, *Up On Cripple Creek*, *Rag Mama Rag*, *The Unfaithful Servant* and most definitely *King Harvest (Has Surely Come)* all invoked a bygone era, when pioneering spirit competed against the elements. For a set using vivid historical observations to respectfully honour America's past, the most curious fact was that 80% of the Band came from Canada. **The Band** was an astonishingly satisfying record, justifying the group's decision to avoid the heavy sounds of the late-sixties, concentrating instead on mellow, beautifully crafted tunes.

(26)

AFTER THE GOLD RUSH – NEIL YOUNG (1970)

(Tell Me Why/After The Gold Rush/Only Love Can Break Your Heart/Southern Man/Till The Morning Comes/Oh Lonesome Me/Don't Let It Bring You Down/Birds/When You Dance I Can Really Love/I Believe In You/Cripple Creek Ferry)

Top Track: Southern Man

Neil Young's faltering solo career after the break-up of Buffalo Springfield was salvaged from the brink by **Everybody Knows This Is Nowhere**. Rather than build on its foundations by pursuing further epic proportioned work, he set in motion an artistic trait for continually proving to be unpredictable. **After The Gold Rush** steered away from the lengthy guitar solos so pronounced on his landmark LP from 1969, homing in on concise sentiments to love, racism and post-Aquarian angst. Recorded at his home in Topanga Canyon, it had originally been planned as a soundtrack to a movie. However, the Dean Stockwell project fell through, leaving Young holding a batch of songs. Using the same name as the aborted screenplay, they collectively became his third solo album, with credit duly given to Stockwell on the back cover.

Tell Me Why set the acoustic tone for much of what followed; a simple composition centred on one man and his guitar, singing cryptic lyrics to the delight of the last surviving hippies. It wasn't until track two that the album really started to make sense. Young mourned for the sixties and warned apocalyptically at the new decade's dawn. Abrupt metaphors were unveiled (burned out basement and new home in the sun) – starkness heightened by scant musical accompaniment that included an unlikely instrument on a rock album - a French horn during the solo. A song split in to three parts, past present and future, it was one of those 'the seventies start here' moments.

The controversial *Southern Man* saw Young passing critical comment on white America's bible-belt bigotry towards blacks. Unpleasant remnants from the previous decade still remained in US society, with the land of equal opportunity and so say justice for all suffering a damning indictment. Lynyrd Skynyrd would, in later years, challenge his views with their slamming verdict on *Sweet Home Alabama*.

More in keeping with the spirit of **After The Gold Rush** was the single, *Only Love Can Break Your Heart*. Young sounded chilled, albeit despondent, on this subdued Folk tune. Only Shakey could conclude both sides to a vital record (vinyl/cassette) with what can best be described as throwaway nonsense and get away with it (*Till The Morning Comes* and *Cripple Creek Ferry* were half-baked and irrelevant). Fortunately, the light-heartedness of their intrusion wasn't unbearable!

Buried amongst the abundance of treasures could be heard stubborn determination (*Don't Let It Bring You Down*), a beautiful ballad (*Birds*), romance (*When You Dance I Can Really Love*) and semi-rock (*I Believe In You*). Young's third LP remains an enigmatic masterpiece that matures with each play.

(27)

THE CLASH (1977)

(Janie Jones/Remote Control/I'm So Bored With The U.S.A./White Riot/Hate & War/What's My Name/ Deny/London's Burning/Career Opportunities/Cheat/ Protex Blue/Police & Thieves/48 Hours/Garageland)

Top Track: White Riot

It's 1976, it's the UK - you had to be there to believe just how bad music had become. A quick glance through the best-selling charts shows that, in comparison with the golden age 1965-72, things were getting seriously stale. No less than 39 weeks were spent at Number 1 by compilations, with Slim Whitman, Glen Campbell and the Beach Boys enjoying sustained durations at the top. Change was urgently needed and had to come from within. Two bands stepped forward grasping the initiative, injecting anger back in to the lethargic animal called rock.

Whereas the Sex Pistols were considered the flagship of British Punk, assisted by their stronger emphasis on courting hard-hitting controversy, it was the Clash that identified closest with the street-level mentality amongst alienated youth. Recorded in spurts during January 1977, **The Clash** condensed in two-minutes thrashing sound-bites, several social/political issues afflicting modern Britain. *Career Opportunities* spoke on behalf of the increasing numbers of unemployed, *I'm So Bored With The U.S.A.* snarled distaste for all-things American, whilst *White Riot* and *London's Burning* illustrated discontent on urban streets. Despite media attention picking-up on the band's Punk antics, there were more than just three chords in their repertoire - *Police & Thieves*, a late addition to the track-listings, showed courage to reach out beyond the immediate Punk hard core by using elements from Reggae.

Whilst the Sex Pistols were driven by intense rock, the Clash were deemed more in tune with the garage philosophy by adopting a cruder, rougher ethos that came straight from the gritty street corner. In the UK their debut was heralded as a pivotal point in rock history. Worthy of note also, far away in America, the conservative Rolling Stone magazine gave strong applause for the LP, commenting on the pure venting of outrage and frustration. Other than on import, however, the record was not available to the US market until 1979. Even then, it was in a dramatically altered running order, tampered by the addition of 'hit' singles. The original UK version from 1977 remains definitive, with every track an anthem for the dispossessed.

(28)

JOHN LENNON/PLASTIC ONO BAND (1970)

(*Mother/Hold On/I Found Out/Working Class Hero/ Isolation/Remember/Love/Well Well Well/Look At Me/ God/My Mummy's Dead*)

Top Track: God

Not even stoned minds in the sixties could comprehend Lennon's tentative 'modernist' collaborations with Yoko Ono. **Unfinished Music No 1: Two Virgins** and **Unfinished Music No 2: Life With The Lions** amounted to nothing more than experimental 'noise'. His first proper releases were far more interesting, although still a difficult, tense experience for millions of fans. The debut 45, *Give Peace A Chance*, was an idealistic, if somewhat head-in-the-clouds naive, mantra plea for a better world. The follow-up, *Cold Turkey*, tilted the attention inwards, providing an important lesson for cravers, a dire warning to those considering experimenting with drugs. If the kaleidoscopic landscape from **Sgt Pepper's Lonely Hearts Club Band** marked the high, *Cold Turkey* acted as a timely reminder of the downside to the hallucinated dreamland.

Instant Karma was the third single, famed for being written and recorded in one day. It was a jovial 45, showing that spontaneity hadn't died out with the advent of meticulous recording techniques. The popular culture of convenience appeared to shelter no boundaries, from fast food to fast cars - so why not instantaneous nirvana? The first real Lennon solo LP arrived in December 1970 and offered a hard pill to swallow for any Beatles fan praying that they were only temporarily splitting-up.

Plastic Ono Band showed no sign of remorse or hope that a reconciliation spirit might prevail. Instead, a very personal theme emerged, drawn from earlier confessional prototypes such as *I'm A Loser*, *In My Life* and *Help!* Prior to the recording sessions, Lennon had been undergoing a relatively new form of psychotherapy, Primal Scream. During treatment he was encouraged to scream loudly, attempting to re-engage with inner-feelings. On the album he did precisely that, on *Mother* screaming his anguish over the death of his mother. The absence of a father figure in his formative years matched this heartache, with a desperate cry for paternal presence. At first it was controlled anger but, by song's end, his traumatised thoughts got the upper-hand, howling for his mother not to go, for Daddy to come home. *Mother* was compelling and bruising but elsewhere there existed a gentle homage to companionship (*Love*) and a commemoration to his unwanted status as the *Working Class Hero*.

In 1970 Lennon declared his independence, sending a clear message that, as a musician and human being, he was looking to the future. It resulted in one conclusion, a painful ending for those clinging to the dream of a Beatles reunion. *God* was a song about... God. At least that's what first impressions suggested but on closer examination it could have been about...? Lennon reeled off a list of fallen heroes. Jesus, Kennedy and Buddha were amongst the name-checked and then he moved in a bit too close for comfort,

Elvis, Zimmerman and... It finished with the icon that he had stopped truly believing in...Beatles. It was the end of the dream. The sixties were over, the hippy era gone, the Beatles gone. As well as being the album's closing song (*My Mummy's Dead* was a pointless ditty), it was Lennon's emphatic full stop to the most popular band of all-time.

(29)

HIGHWAY 61 REVISITED – BOB DYLAN (1965)

(*Like A Rolling Stone/Tombstone Blues/It Takes A Lot To Laugh, It Takes A Train To Cry/From A Buick 6/Ballad Of A Thin Man/Queen Jane Approximately/Highway 61 Revisited/Just Like Tom Thumb's Blues/Desolation Row*)

Top Track: *Like A Rolling Stone*

Becoming the Folk scene's champion was an awkward crown to wear for Minnesota's favourite son. Despite a poor-selling debut in 1962, further Woody Guthrie inspired records propelled Dylan to the forefront, a status consolidated by generation-defining protest anthems, *Blowin' In The Wind*, *A Hard Rain's A-Gonna Fall* and *The Times They Are A-Changin'*. Whilst the pop business continued to plug repetitive tunes obtained from youthful love experiences, Dylan searched beyond superficial emotions, spotlighting intellectual issues connected to the social and political world. Conflict had been a good source for written material but in 1965 he unwittingly became the instigator of civil war within the Folk fraternity.

His fifth LP, **Bringing It All Back Home**, was effectively split in to two definitive halves - Side 1 embraced rock-infusion via electrification, Side 2 complied with more traditional Folk tastes. In doing so, it cast him firmly in the role of thinking man's alternative to the superficiality personified by pop. The new direction was seismic, with an incisive push towards immediate accessibility (*Subterranean Homesick Blues* and *Maggie's Farm*), counter-balanced by easy-going melodies (*Mr Tambourine Man* and *It's All Over Now, Baby Blue*). The upward gear change, however, was dwarfed in comparison with the meteoric shift on his next instalment, **Highway 61 Revisited**.

Like A Rolling Stone, arguably the greatest 45 of all-time, smashed through many stubborn barriers. At over six minutes, there were clearly logistical problems posed for radio programmers accustomed to predictable familiarity via pop's sub-three minutes formula. Equally, the subject matter strayed from conventional wisdom's belief for playing things safe, with Dylan firing-off a barrage of seething resentment, but aimed at whom? It's a question that, to this day, continues to ignite healthy debate - Joan Baez, Edie Sedgwick, or perhaps bitterness targeted at himself? The song was layered with sufficient surrealism to render it virtually impossible to identify just one specific suspect. Unquestionably, however, it was a breakthrough 45 in musical history (you only have to sample 1965's pop charts to hear why), creating further tidal waves of apprehension amongst Folk diehards. Where was Dylan taking the genre and, more so, how far out were the limits going?

There was no escaping from the fact that he was looking for new quarters to harbour his extensive lyrical vocabulary. Through stormy numbers such as *Tombstone Blues*, the folk/blues-laced *It Takes A Lot To Laugh, It Takes A Train To Cry* and *Ballad Of A Thin Man*, Dylan found the perfect home. By the time we reach *Queen Jane Approximately* most weak-hearted Folk disciples had left the room, spitting their fury at the floor as they departed.

They should have stayed the distance, for a big album warranted a fitting finish - at 11:21 minutes, finales didn't get much bigger than *Desolation Row*. The huge canvas afforded him scope to roll-call through a lengthy procession of famous personalities (Cinderella, Bette Davis, Romeo, Ophelia...) imaginatively linked by a lost hope theme. Enigmatically, given his surge towards rock, here was a Folk tune to the core, heavily flavoured with harmonica support and acoustic guitar strummed with determined commitment. The lyrics dwelled at length over an overwhelming feeling of impending decline – a gloomy message that Folk devotees should have heeded. **Highway 61 Revisited** was the greatest LP of all-time upon its release in 1965 - an honour that lasted less than a year, due to the continued progression by both Dylan and his main competitors.

(30)

DEFINITELY MAYBE – OASIS (1994)

(*Rock 'n' Roll Star/Shakermaker/Live Forever/Up In The Sky/Columbia/Supersonic/Bring It On Down/Cigarettes & Alcohol/Digsy's Dinner/Slide Away/Married With Children*)

Top Track: Rock 'n' Roll Star

The opening statement on **Definitely Maybe** left no uncertainty of their huge ambition. Riffs that sparked flashbacks to the Sex Pistols boomed from the loudspeakers as Liam Gallagher howled his rock 'n' roll dream. Oozing with attitude, it was evident UK music was in for a major wake-up call. Not since the Stone Roses had Britain heralded a guitar band with so much promise, so much belief in their ability to do better than the rest.

They set the target to beat with track 1 from album 1, but it dawned soon after that originality wasn't going to be their strong point. *Shakermaker* was nothing more than a sneering update of a tune that originated in a famous advertisement for Coca-Cola (re-worked by the New Seekers as *I'd Like To Teach The World To Sing*). Oasis were subsequently successfully sued, prompting Noel Gallagher to comment that they now drank Pepsi!

Artistic credibility was restored on *Live Forever*, a song understood by the disgruntled, post-Grunge generation and, for many, was the album's highpoint. Oasis stand accused of borrowing from the Beatles and, some might say, it began here, but on their debut establishing a precise source of inspirational influence wasn't easy. Who, for example, lay in their thoughts on *Up In The Sky* (the Fab Four on speed maybe), the roughened tension of *Columbia* or the first-class rocker *Bring It On Down*? *Cigarettes & Alcohol* started off sounding like *Get It On* by seventies glam rockers T.Rex, only to be hijacked by Liam's re-enactment of Mr Rotten's Punk attitude. Meanwhile, *Slide Away* witnessed a strange kind of crossover between John Lennon and Neil Young. In amongst its suspending chords that delightfully lingered, Oasis offered unrelenting passion.

Concluding with the out of context, self-fulfilling prophecy, *Married With Children*, **Definitely Maybe** combined old with a little bit of new, concocting a potent cocktail that placed the band at the top of British rock in the nineties. Noel confessed that the intention was to make the most important record since **Nevermind**. Passing time has done little damage to its reputation and, if anything, they most definitely succeeded in their aim. Often classified as Brit Pop's answer to **Never Mind The Bollocks Here's The Sex Pistols**, such assessments are viewed as flattery by the old-school but, in truth, it was a welcome reminder of rock's enduring qualities.

(31)

AUTOMATIC FOR THE PEOPLE – R.E.M. (1992)

(*Drive/Try Not To Breathe/The Sidewinder Sleeps Tonite/ Everybody Hurts/New Orleans Instrumental Number 1/ Sweetness Follows/Monty Got A Raw Deal/Ignoreland/Star Me Kitten/Man On The Moon/Nightswimming/Find The River*)

Top Track: Man On The Moon

During the mid-eighties to early-nineties R.E.M. made more superb songs than any other American 'alternative' band. From a humble beginning with the release of the *Chronic Town* EP in 1982, **Murmur** (1983), **Lifes Rich Pageant** (1986), **Green** (1988) and **Out Of Time** (1991) demonstrated a canny knack for building upon the strengths of preceding work. During that period they transformed from a band with campus-based support to a multi-national, arena-packing major player on the rock stage, with devoted fans in awe of their quirky, meaningful sound.

In 1992 came their undisputed career highpoint. Their albums usually began on a positive, up-beat note but not on this occasion. Instead of *Radio Free Europe* or *Pop Song '89* there was *Drive*, a mellow pedestrian-paced tune that, dissimilar to previous R.E.M. tracks, veered towards Folk music. The sedate momentum coated with dark, morbid lyrics, defined **Automatic For The People**, with few audible indications of a *Stand* or *Shiny Happy People*. The restrained pain felt on *Everybody Hurts* carried a universal message, although beneath the surface there existed slender hope that no matter how bad life gets, things can always improve. A song marginally offering optimism and empathy, few can fail to be moved by its powerful impact. No doubt too, it has prevented several suicides.

There were spells of ill-fitting ease, *The Sidewinder Sleeps Tonite* particularly, but the album's axis rested on the earthliness of simple acoustic melodies (*Drive* and *Try Not To Breathe*), uplifting periods of euphoric harmonies (*Find The River*) and the celebrative controversy surrounding the conspiracy theories about the fake moon landings (*Man On The Moon*).

Whilst mainstream music fans during 1992 either rocked to pretentious US Punk rock or blew their minds out raving in a derelict warehouse, R.E.M. offered a richly rewarding alternative. Given America's overheating fixation with deep bass heaviness saturated with foreboding lyrics, paradoxically the best US album released during the year symbolised the antithesis of Grunge.

(32)

FOREVER CHANGES – LOVE (1967)

(***Alone Again Or/A House Is Not A Motel/ Andmoreagain/The Daily Planet/Old Man/The Red Telephone/Maybe The People Would Be The Times Or Between Clark And Hilldale/Live And Let Live/The Good Humor Man He Sees Everything Like This/ Bummer In The Summer/You Set The*** Scene)

Top Track: Alone Again Or

Arthur Lee assessed on *Alone Again Or* that he could love almost everyone. It typified hippy ideology but this beautiful song, glistening with Spanish styled guitars and brass orchestrations, also hid few reservations about loneliness in a peace and love utopia. Popular misconceptions that the Summer of Love generation lived in drug-induced bliss were further brought into doubt on *A House Is Not A Motel*. *Andmoreagain* continued the deflated rhetoric, with further revelations of sadness. The opening trio were highly representative of a set blossoming with schizoid brilliance, majestic arrangements and aural wonders. *Old Man, The Red Telephone, Live*

And Let Live and *You Set The Scene* also bloomed with flower-power aromas.

Love was a stereotypical tag for a group from the hippy era but, in reality, they were love in name only. The sessions for their masterpiece were dogged with ill-feeling, hindered by stoned band members and disagreements over how the music should sound. Bryan Maclean, the author of *Alone Again Or*, was reported to be dissatisfied with the final vocals, Lee meanwhile, was reluctant to the inclusion of fanciful arrangements of any kind. It made for an uncomfortable environment in which to concoct such delicate compositions. Perhaps this explains why so much that can be heard feels disjointed, splintering at the edges, but somehow held together by a force stronger than the sum of the individual components.

Blending youthful innocence and high moral considerations for mankind, **Forever Changes** captures the Summer of Love spirit like no other. Released just as dusk began to settle on 1967, this is very much a record of its time. The highly colourful LP cover could only come from this year, likewise the misguided and generous belief in humanity pervaded by the songs.

(33)
VOL 4 – BLACK SABBATH (1972)

(***Wheels Of Confusion / Tomorrow's Dream / Changes/ FX/ Supernaut / Snowblind/Cornucopia/Laguna Sunrise/St Vitus Dance/Under The Sun***)

Top Track: Supernaut

Music historians often recall the innovation achieved by British psychedelic experimenters (Pink Floyd), Heavy Metal specialists (Led Zeppelin) and even the pomp excesses typified by Yes and Emerson, Lake & Palmer. For too long, the same level of recognition wasn't granted to one of the greatest pioneers of them all. Black Sabbath (Ozzy Osbourne, Tony Iommi, Geezer Butler and Bill Ward) originated from the industrialised Black Country during the late-sixties, imposing a unique brand of hook-driven rock on an unsuspecting world. Their debut LP, together with the groundbreaking follow-up, **Paranoid**, formed the blueprint of a style that served them well throughout the seventies. The songs were built around memorable guitar riffs, whilst lyrical themes explored sinister topics such as occultism, with mental instability thrown in adding a crazed element.

Although **Paranoid** gets the thumbs up with critics and heavies (due to the hit 45 and also the titanic opener *War Pigs*), it was on their misunderstood fourth set that they reached a zenith. **Vol 4** covered everything from head-banging nuggets, through to fancy recording trickery, classical orchestrations, pianos and Spanish guitars. Inevitably, the heavy stuff dominated as Iommi's riff-mastery developed genius proportions.

Wheels Of Confusion was an eight minutes tour-de-force wallowing in self-pitiful woe, that began in a land of fairy tales and innocence. It was a harmless start but hardly a lullaby dedication to happier days. The track's tempo quickened to fever pitch culminating in purity being overcome by darker forces. Modern head-bangers unfamiliar with this track should put aside any Black Sabbath misgivings and give it a go – you'll love it.

Tomorrow's Dream continued with the riffs and hooks but, at just short of three minutes, was less damaging on twitchy nerves. The song's fit-to-size measurements, assisted by a sugar-coated commercialised tune, resulted in a minor hit 45, their first since *Paranoid*. Out of character with anything that they had done before the piano ballad, *Changes*, lightened the mood but upset the rock fundamentalists. It's at this point where **Vol 4** prompts mixed responses – was it a betrayal of HM or brave audacity to try something different?

The truly head-spinning *Supernaut* brought Side One to a heart-thumping conclusion. The electric guitar began to roar, Ward went totally mental on the drums and Ozzy shrieked like his life depended on it. If ever there was the perfect song for that age-old ritual of air-guitar tomfoolery, this was it. Move breakable furniture to a safe distance, tell the neighbours to leave the country and play *Supernaut* destructively loud - it's what the loudspeakers and bass boomers were put on earth for. They signed-off this classic with a declaration that they were leaving the future behind - how true too, as Black Sabbath's ethos for the remainder of Ozzy's tenure as lead singer fluctuated little from the path of straight rock.

On *Snowblind* the consequences of cocaine addiction were analysed with revealing insight. Coked-up addicts and rock fanatics could unite for this, even if its biggest hook wasn't the white powder but the dazzling tune within a tune technique (check out also *Cornucopia* and *St Vitus Dance* for similar ideas). ***Vol 4*** was undervalued in its time, with commentators pouring scorn on its dense, sludge sound but interest has since been relit as a direct result of the late-eighties Grunge movement.

(34)

MOON SAFARI – AIR (1998)

(*La Femme D'Argent/Sexy Boy/All I Need/Kelly Watch The Stars/Talisman/Remember/You Make It Easy/Ce Matin-La/New Star In The Sky/Le Voyage De Penelope*)

Top Track: *La Femme D'Argent*

Coming from Versailles, Paris was a duo keen to have relaxing fun with instrumentations. Jean-Benoit Dunckel and Nicolas Godin were from the same French Electronica wave as Daft Punk but the music they had in mind couldn't have been further removed. Whereas Messrs Bangalter and Homem-Christo pursued disco-stomping beats, Air floated transcendentally in an alternative chill-out zone. The debut single, *Modular Mix*, subsequently proved to be one of their snappier tunes and yet, even this classy slice of jazzy pop glided with polished grace. Further minor hits followed but it wasn't until **Moon Safari** that their true hypnotic potential was realised.

Proudly displaying their origins on the album sleeve - Air French Band – some tracks had Gallic titles, *La Femme D'Argent*, *Ce Matin-La* and *Le Voyage De Penelope*. Had the time come for a mainland European language to be taken seriously in the world of contemporary music? Alas non! Four of the ten songs were instrumentals but, nevertheless, expressed emotions better than words could ever. The elongated bass lines on *Talisman* inspired memories of the late-sixties, a decade that they also turned to for the shortest track. Admitting that they weren't immune to the occasional sampling, Air did it in joyous style with *Remember* (lifting the drum beat from the Beach Boys' 1968 pop gem *Do It Again*). In the land resided in by **Moon Safari** everything was happy and at peace with its surroundings. Words were superfluous, its agenda more to do with re-capturing pleasantries, long-lost charms and sweet innocence.

Enjoy slight electro Jazz (*La Femme D'Argent*), surreal Parisian Folk (*All I Need*), mellowing kitsch (*Le Voyage De Penelope*) and sheer serenity, *New Star In The Sky*. Hit singles, *Sexy Boy* and *Kelly Watch The Stars*, are serious contenders for best '45s' of the nineties, but the album is also home to some adorably beautiful tunes. For sure, at a time when the world began to suffer from media-hyped fixation with pre-millennium tension, **Moon Safari** was a wonderful antidote to pressurised, modern-day living. Those unfamiliar with its beneficial qualities should try it – as an alternative to cracking open a bottle of wine at the end of a bad day, listen to this instead and feel your anxieties slip away.

100 GREAT ALBUM TRACKS 1970-79

1. STAIRWAY TO HEAVEN (**LED ZEPPELIN IV**) – LED ZEPPELIN 1971
2. TIME (**DARK SIDE OF THE MOON**) - PINK FLOYD 1973
3. SOUTHERN MAN (**AFTER THE GOLD RUSH**) – NEIL YOUNG 1970
4. ANARCHY IN THE UK (**NEVER MIND THE BOLLOCKS HERE'S THE SEX PISTOLS**) – SEX PISTOLS 1977
5. MARQUEE MOON (**MARQUEE MOON**) – TELEVISION 1977
6. BORN TO RUN (**BORN TO RUN**) – BRUCE SPRINGSTEEN 1975
7. LONDON CALLING (**LONDON CALLING**) – THE CLASH 1979
8. DISORDER (**UNKNOWN PLEASURES**) – JOY DIVISION 1979
9. AT THE CHIME OF A CITY CLOCK (**BRYTER LAYTER**) - NICK DRAKE 1970
10. RETURN OF THE GRIEVOUS ANGEL (**GRIEVOUS ANGEL**) – GRAM PARSONS 1974
11. IMAGINE (**IMAGINE**) - JOHN LENNON 1971
12. WILLIN' (**SAILIN' SHOES**) - LITTLE FEAT 1972
13. INTO THE MYSTIC (**MOONDANCE**) – VAN MORRISON 1970
14. SUPERNAUT (**VOL 4**) - BLACK SABBATH 1972
15. STARMAN (**THE RISE AND FALL OF ZIGGY STARDUST AND THE SPIDERS FROM MARS**) – DAVID BOWIE 1972
16. BROWN SUGAR (**STICKY FINGERS**) – THE ROLLING STONES 1971

17	WALK ON THE WILD SIDE (**TRANSFORMER**) – LOU REED 1972	
18	LAYLA (**LAYLA AND OTHER ASSORTED LOVE SONGS**) – DEREK & THE DOMINOS 1970	
19	CHILD IN TIME (**DEEP PURPLE IN ROCK**) – DEEP PURPLE 1970	
20	HAPPY (**EXILE ON MAIN STREET**) – THE ROLLING STONES 1972	
21	SWEET HOME ALABAMA (**SECOND HELPING**) – LYNYRD SKYNYRD 1974	
22	IMMIGRANT SONG (**LED ZEPPELIN III**) – LED ZEPPELIN 1970	
23	RIDERS ON THE STORM (**L.A. WOMAN**) – THE DOORS 1971	
24	GLORIA (**HORSES**) - PATTI SMITH 1975	
25	WON'T GET FOOLED AGAIN (**WHO'S NEXT**) – THE WHO 1971	
26	AUTOBAHN (**AUTOBAHN**) - KRAFTWERK 1974	
27	SHINE ON YOU CRAZY DIAMOND (PARTS 1-5) (**WISH YOU WERE HERE**) - PINK FLOYD 1975	
28	I WISH (**SONGS IN THE KEY OF LIFE**) – STEVIE WONDER 1976	
29	I WANT TO SEE THE BRIGHT LIGHTS TONIGHT (**I WANT TO SEE THE BRIGHT LIGHTS TONIGHT**) – RICHARD & LINDA THOMPSON 1974	
30	TAKE ME TO THE RIVER (**MORE SONGS ABOUT BUILDINGS AND FOOD**) – TALKING HEADS 1978	
31	TEENAGE KICKS (**THE UNDERTONES**) – THE UNDERTONES 1979	
32	SHAKE SOME ACTION (**SHAKE SOME ACTION**) - FLAMIN' GROOVIES 1976	

33	WHO'LL STOP THE RAIN (**COSMO'S FACTORY**) – CREEDENCE CLEARWATER REVIVAL 1970	
34	LISTEN TO THE LION (**SAINT DOMINIC'S PREVIEW**) – VAN MORRISON 1972	
35	GOD SAVE THE QUEEN (**NEVER MIND THE BOLLOCKS HERE'S THE SEX PISTOLS**) – SEX PISTOLS 1977	
36	ANTHRAX (**ENTERTAINMENT!**) – GANG OF FOUR 1979	
37	THE LAST TIME I SAW RICHARD (**BLUE**) – JONI MITCHELL 1971	
38	GOD (**JOHN LENNON/PLASTIC ONO BAND**) – JOHN LENNON/PLASTIC ONO BAND 1970	
39	PUMP IT UP (**THIS YEAR'S MODEL**) - ELVIS COSTELLO & THE ATTRACTIONS 1978	
40	ROCK 'N' ROLL (**LED ZEPPELIN IV**) – LED ZEPPELIN 1971	
41	HEART OF THE SUNRISE (**FRAGILE**) – YES 1971	
42	SHE'S LOST CONTROL (**UNKNOWN PLEASURES**) – JOY DIVISION 1979	
43	INNER CITY BLUES (MAKE ME WANNA HOLLER) (**WHAT'S GOING ON**) – MARVIN GAYE 1971	
44	BRIDGE OVER TROUBLED WATER (**BRIDGE OVER TROUBLED WATER**) – SIMON & GARFUNKEL 1970	
45	STREET LIFE (**STRANDED**) – ROXY MUSIC 1973	
46	O MY SOUL (**RADIO CITY**) – BIG STAR 1974	
47	IN MY TIME OF DYING (**PHYSICAL GRAFFITI**) – LED ZEPPELIN 1975	
48	LIKE A HURRICANE (**AMERICAN STARS 'N BARS**) – NEIL YOUNG 1977	
49	TANGLED UP IN BLUE (**BLOOD ON THE TRACKS**) – BOB DYLAN 1975	

50	GO YOUR OWN WAY (**RUMOURS**) – FLEETWOOD MAC 1977	
51	ALL THE YOUNG DUDES (**ALL THE YOUNG DUDES**) – MOTT THE HOOPLE 1972	
52	SWALLOW MY PRIDE (**LEAVE HOME**) – THE RAMONES 1977	
53	I SHOT THE SHERIFF (**461 OCEAN BOULEVARD**) – ERIC CLAPTON 1974	
54	COMFORTABLY NUMB (**THE WALL**) – PINK FLOYD 1979	
55	SURF'S UP (**SURF'S UP**) – THE BEACH BOYS 1971	
56	ROADRUNNER (**THE MODERN LOVERS**) – THE MODERN LOVERS 1976	
57	SOUND AND VISION (**LOW**) – DAVID BOWIE 1977	
58	ROCK & ROLL (**LOADED**) – THE VELVET UNDERGROUND 1970	
59	BLUES IN D (**KATE & ANNA MCGARRIGLE**) – KATE & ANNA MCGARRIGLE 1976	
60	TEACH YOUR CHILDREN (**DEJA VU**) – CROSBY, STILLS, NASH & YOUNG 1970	
61	HEART OF GLASS (**PARALLEL LINES**) – BLONDIE 1978	
62	TRANS-EUROPE EXPRESS (**TRANS-EUROPE EXPRESS**) – KRAFTWERK 1977	
63	RUNNIN' WITH THE DEVIL (**VAN HALEN**) – VAN HALEN 1978	
64	DOWN IN THE TUBE STATION AT MIDNIGHT (**ALL MOD CONS**) – THE JAM 1978	
65	MANDOLIN WIND (**EVERY PICTURE TELLS A STORY**) – ROD STEWART 1971	
66	PERSONALITY CRISIS (**NEW YORK DOLLS**) - NEW YORK DOLLS 1973	

67   LONG TRAIN RUNNIN' (**THE CAPTAIN AND ME**) - THE DOOBIE BROTHERS 1973

68   SPACE STATION NO 5 (**MONTROSE**) – MONTROSE 1973

69   REELIN' IN THE YEARS (**CAN'T BUY A THRILL**) – STEELY DAN 1972

70   BAND ON THE RUN (**BAND ON THE RUN**) – PAUL McCARTNEY & WINGS 1973

71   WHEN THE LEVEE BREAKS (**LED ZEPPELIN IV**) – LED ZEPPELIN 1971

72   WAITIN' FOR THE BUS (**TRES HOMBRES**) – ZZ TOP 1973

73   ISN'T IT A PITY (**ALL THINGS MUST PASS**) – GEORGE HARRISON 1970

74   ONE OF THESE NIGHTS (**ONE OF THESE NIGHTS**) – THE EAGLES 1975

75   NO WOMAN, NO CRY (**NATTY DREAD**) - BOB MARLEY & THE WAILERS 1974

76   YOU AIN'T SEEN NOTHING YET (**NOT FRAGILE**) – BACHMAN-TURNER OVERDRIVE 1974

77   SINGING WINDS, CRYING BEASTS (**ABRAXAS**) – SANTANA 1970

78   DOWN PAYMENT BLUES (**POWERAGE**) – AC/DC 1978

79   WISHING WELL (**HEARTBREAKER**) – FREE 1973

80   DON'T ASK ME QUESTIONS (**HOWLIN' WIND**) – GRAHAM PARKER & THE RUMOUR 1976

81   MORE THAN A FEELING (**BOSTON**) – BOSTON 1976

82   GONE DEAD TRAIN (**CRAZY HORSE**) – CRAZY HORSE 1971

83   BOHEMIAN RHAPSODY (**A NIGHT AT THE OPERA**) – QUEEN 1975

84   FLYIN' AWAY (**JOHN FOGERTY**) – JOHN FOGERTY 1975

85   JAILBREAK (**JAILBREAK**) – THIN LIZZY 1976

86   (DON'T FEAR) THE REAPER (**AGENTS OF FORTUNE**) – BLUE OYSTER CULT 1976

87   HOCUS POCUS (**MOVING WAVES**) - FOCUS 1971

88   MESSAGE IN A BOTTLE (**REGGATTA DE BLANC**) – THE POLICE 1979

89   A MESSAGE TO YOU RUDY (**SPECIALS**) – THE SPECIALS 1979

90   LIFE ON MARS? (**HUNKY DORY**) – DAVID BOWIE 1971

91   LOVE LIES BLEEDING (**GOODBYE YELLOW BRICK ROAD**) – ELTON JOHN 1973

92   AMERICAN PIE (**AMERICAN PIE**) – DON MCLEAN 1971

93   THIRTEEN (**#1 RECORD**) – BIG STAR 1972

94   SABBATH BLOODY SABBATH (**SABBATH BLOODY SABBATH**) – BLACK SABBATH 1973

95   AT SEVENTEEN (**BETWEEN THE LINES**) – JANIS IAN 1975

96   THE STRANGER (**THE STRANGER**) - BILLY JOEL 1977

97   BRIGHTON ROCK (**SHEER HEART ATTACK**) - QUEEN 1974

98   SERENADE (**FLY LIKE AN EAGLE**) – STEVE MILLER BAND 1976

99   GONE HOLLYWOOD (**BREAKFAST IN AMERICA**) – SUPERTRAMP 1979

100 I KNOW WHAT I LIKE (IN YOUR WARDROBE) (**SELLING ENGLAND BY THE POUND**) – GENESIS 1973

(35)

WISH YOU WERE HERE – PINK FLOYD (1975)

(Shine On You Crazy Diamond (Parts 1-5)/Welcome To The Machine/Have A Cigar/Wish You Were Here/Shine On You Crazy Diamond (Parts 6-9))

Top Track: Shine On You Crazy Diamond (Parts 1-5)

Whilst they were working on the follow-up to **Dark Side Of The Moon** an overweight, balding and somewhat dishevelled man walked in to the Abbey Road studios, seemingly interested in how things were going for Pink Floyd. Not long after his unannounced entrance, he turned around and walked out, leaving few clues as to the purpose of his impromptu visit. This mysterious character was their long-lost friend and former member, Syd Barrett. The man who made a vital contribution to their initial success had, for no apparent reason, chosen this time to resurface from self-imposed exile, after years of conspicuous absence. The brief encounter transfixed the band, transforming in to a centre of gravity in their thought process, a presence that weighed heavily during the remaining sessions.

The magnitude of its predecessor meant **Wish You Were Here** was predestined to feel dwarfed. Avoiding the easy option of re-writing a winning formula, they tackled the project with clearly different ideas. This time there were no thumping heartbeats and insane voices, no cash registers and orgasmic cries. *Shine On You Crazy Diamond* progressed from an unassuming introduction into a tumultuous joy, breezing through the air with majestic grace. David Gilmour's rapturous, tower-high guitar solos were sequenced immaculately with Dick Parry's saxophone. The net result was a stunning example of contrasting instruments coming together for the good of music. The song, first performed during 1974, celebrated Syd's life, with emphasis on his tragic downfall. Drug abuse and a mental disposition had brought his recording career within the context of Pink Floyd to an abrupt end. His life and the direction that the band took following his departure in 1968 changed forever.

Endless commitments to gruelling tour schedules, together with keeping the record company executives happy, meant that the rock 'n' roll lifestyle wasn't luxuriously full of four star daydreams and Lear jets. It began to feel they were no longer in control of their destiny, merely becoming a small part of the corporate jigsaw. *Welcome To The Machine*, with its opening synthetic engine-room soundtrack, explored this theme with cynical contempt. Later they exposed rock star excessiveness on *Have A Cigar*, summarising with some lyrically cutting remarks.

The LP sleeve portrayed two business men shaking hands, with further 'meaningful' photographs depicting the elements found within the cover. The real significance was heard in the music, for Pink Floyd had risen to the challenge, by matching their previous excursion into paranoia and emotional breakdown.

(36)

I WANT TO SEE THE BRIGHT LIGHTS TONIGHT – RICHARD & LINDA THOMPSON (1974)

(*When I Get To The Border/The Calvary Cross/Withered And Died/I Want To See The Bright Lights Tonight/Down Where The Drunkards Roll/We Sing Hallelujah/Has He Got A Friend For Me/The Little Beggar Girl/The End Of The Rainbow/The Great Valerio*)

Top Track: *I Want To See The Bright Lights Tonight*

Richard Thompson had already left his permanent mark on British music with Fairport Convention. It would be using the same generous spirit for delving into England's Folk legacy that he completed his first release with wife, Linda, **I Want To See The Bright Lights Tonight**. Their songs painted a dark, depressed perspective on the world, cold and damp, poor and dejected with a necessity for escape. On *When I Get To The Border* a man desires starting afresh somewhere else, anywhere will do. On the gorgeous title-track (easily the most commercially accessible moment) avoidance of reality was pursued by simply enjoying a drunken night out.

It was an identifiable need for small pleasures in amongst a mundane existence that brought these songs to life. Unsavoury characters from society's basement (vagabonds and prostitutes) were acknowledged and glorified as everyday heroes, salt of the earth saviours deserving respect. Seldom had a beggar's life been so glowingly celebrated than on *The Little Beggar Girl*, with humble satisfaction derived from taking money off the rich. Ultimately, it's the world's imposing gravity that conquers all attempts to overcome adversity through resilience, with resigned defeat defining *Withered And Died*. Bleaker conclusions followed on *The End Of The Rainbow* and a realisation that life offered nothing worth growing-up for.

This brutally honest LP was applauded by critics but sold few copies during the early years, presumably purchased by the few remaining Folk fans. It wasn't released in America for another two years but the delay did little harm to a set that positively sounded ancient already. These ten beautiful songs were a proud tribute to English Folk music's strength, not just during the final decades of the 20th Century, but over the last few hundred years. Husband and wife duos rarely magic a masterpiece, but on this occasion marital harmony worked together creating a truly special partnership. As with many marriages, it wouldn't last...

(37)

LEAVE HOME – THE RAMONES (1977)

(*Glad To See You Go/Gimme Gimme Shock Treatment/I Remember You/Oh, Oh, I Love Her So/Carbona Not Glue/ Suzy Is A Headbanger/Pinhead/Now I Wanna Be A Good Boy/Swallow My Pride/What's Your Game/California Sun/ Commando/You're Gonna Kill That Girl/You Should Never Have Opened That Door*)

Top Track: Swallow My Pride

Their outrageously basic debut turned the clocks back to rock 'n' roll's formative years. *Blitzkrieg Bop*, *Judy Is A Punk*, *Chain Saw* and *Now I Wanna Sniff Some Glue* (collectively lasting seven minutes) were representative of a challenge to the mid-seventies norm for sophisticated production and intricate song structures. **The Ramones** is usually regarded as their definitive record, however **Leave Home** enhanced a minimal chords/few verses dynamics by adding layers of pop flavourings. The result was a Punk/New Wave/Pop classic.

Their mastery of efficient, sub-three minutes tunes was crafted from several years experience, with the notable influence of the early-sixties US surf scene. *Oh, Oh, I Love Her So, California Sun* and *I Remember You* fused New Wave's energy with sunny Beach Boys harmonies, formulising an addiction that made repeatedly playing this LP a compulsive pastime. The band's best work can be found here, including crowd pleasers *Suzy Is A Headbanger, Swallow My Pride* and *Pinhead*. Several times the lyrics used US jargon that induced a bemused response from a British audience. Who or what were pinheads, geeks and headbangers? It all added to a fascination with a band that stood out from the pack.

Gruesome storylines unfolded, with references to Charles Manson (*Glad To See You Go*), psychologically cracking (*Gimme Gimme Shock Treatment*) and wanton murder (*You're Gonna Kill That Girl*). Dry humour finished the album on a whimsical note by chopping a head off with an axe (*You Should Never Have Opened That Door*). These were not songs for the easily offended or, for that matter, anyone that couldn't see the funny side to a warped perspective on life.

Leave Home contained 14 tracks, but lasted just 31 minutes. They flashed by so fast it was time to put the stylus back to the start and play again before you knew it. So simple, a few guitar chords, a small handful of lyrics, no fillers, no excessive solos (were there any solos?). In essence, anybody could make this sound – the very reason Punk was so vital.

(38)

RUMOURS – FLEETWOOD MAC (1977)

(*Second Hand News/Dreams/Never Going Back Again/ Don't Stop/Go Your Own Way/Songbird/The Chain/You Make Loving Fun/I Don't Want To Know/Oh Daddy/Gold Dust Woman*)

Top Track: *Go Your Own Way*

There may have been revolution in the air during 1977, but there were few commercial signs of this. Standing in the face of Punk's challenge, offering an album of finely-tuned compositions entwined with tales of marital discord, Fleetwood Mac stayed at the top of US charts for over six months. Unlike Punk's coarse rhetoric, **Rumours** overflowed with delicate, meaningful lyrics derived from personal woes. Both relationships within the band (John & Christine McVie and Lindsey Buckingham & Stevie Nicks) had hit rocky ground. Their separations made for an awkward time in the studios, providing the catalyst for the unleashing of strong emotions.

Second Hand News was a jaunty introduction (musically), but Buckingham wasted little time in setting free vented feelings, making clear he was not going to miss his former partner. Nicks' *Dreams* appeared to grasp hope from despair, suggesting that freedom from an ailing relationship wasn't necessarily the way forward. *Don't Stop* pushed optimism to the fore, with a wish to forget the bitter past and be positive for tomorrow - a sentiment echoed by many divorced couples re-building their lives. It was a constructive message but, at times isolated, weighed down by regrets and distrust.

Go Your Own Way put things back on an even keel, with further outbursts, specifically intended by Buckingham at Nicks. Despite her protests, an unflattering lyric remained unedited. In doing so, it mirrored angry feuding between two broken-hearted lovers plummeting through their darkest hours. More cryptic revelations were to follow, the bouncy *You Make Loving Fun* (referring to an extra-marital affair) and *Gold Dust Woman* (Nicks' drug problems?). Several 45s were released but, 'hidden away' on **Rumours**, *Never Going Back Again*, *The Chain* (featuring one of the all-time great bass licks) and *Oh Daddy* (a tribute to the band's hub, Mick Fleetwood?) deserve greater recognition.

(39)

BRIDGE OVER TROUBLED WATER – SIMON & GARFUNKEL (1970)

(*Bridge Over Troubled Water/El Condor Pasa/Cecilia/Keep The Customer Satisfied/So Long, Frank Lloyd Wright/The Boxer/Baby Driver/The Only Living Boy In New York/Why Don't You Write Me/Bye Bye Love/Song For The Asking*)

Top Track: Bridge Over Troubled Water

Simon & Garfunkel spent much of their time during the sixties touring in England. One famous story has it that the lyrics to their 1966 hit, *Homeward Bound*, were penned whilst Paul Simon was waiting for a train in Widnes. Another yarn from rock folklore stated that he gained inspiration for the words to *Bridge Over Troubled Water* during a visit to Devon.

A brief visit to Bickleigh, a small village four miles from Tiverton, makes it understandable why the song's lyrical tilt towards vulnerable loneliness could have been written here. The River Exe gushes forcefully through as a bridge stands dutifully on guard, providing a safe crossing. For sure it's a picture postcard landmark, but as for its place in rock history? The rumours surrounding the song's origins were allegedly initiated by an imaginative journalist, with Simon several years later confirming a hymn had really been his main influence. Hymn or bridge, without doubt the lyrics carried an uplifting renewable spirit, a comforting source of hope for the friendless in difficult times. Art Garfunkel's intelligent vocal translation, together with an inspired piano arrangement, made for a winning combination.

The duo's final studio LP, in magpie fashion, gathered a gleaming assortment of musical genres. The title-track's Gospel introduction gave way to the Peruvian flavoured, *El Condor Pasa*, lyrically decorated with readily appreciated messages. Next up came the mildly raunchy *Cecilia* (a man climbs out of bed to wash his face, only to discover on his return his place taken by someone else) - very late-sixties!

Simon and Garfunkel were defined by their harmonies which, for astute listeners, were reminiscent of fifties legends the Everly Brothers. Fittingly, the sixties equivalents recorded a live take of *Bye Bye Love*. The sessions for the album, however, were anything but harmonious, with Garfunkel absent for considerable periods making a film, far away in Mexico. Simon was left to complete the songs, with painstaking hours spent on producing the perfect sound. *Baby Driver*, *Keep The Customer Satisfied*, *The Only Living Boy In New York* and *The Boxer* (a hit from '68) were superb examples of a partnership reaching an artistic peak. They split shortly afterwards - a sign of the times, when rock groups were breaking-up and iconic stars were paying the ultimate price.

(40)

TUBULAR BELLS – MIKE OLDFIELD (1973)

(Tubular Bells Part One/Tubular Bells Part Two)

Top Track: *Tubular Bells Part One*

Giving away free posters and lyric sheets with an LP was a widespread practice during the late-sixties/early-seventies. One album in 1973 that didn't provide a lyric sheet was Mike Oldfield's ***Tubular Bells***, for one very simple reason - there were no lyrics. The only words came from Master of Ceremonies, Viv Stanshall, roll-calling some of the instruments used in the album's making. Other than drums, played by Steve Broughton, it was essentially a one-man band with Oldfield playing virtually everything. As Stanshall testified, this ranged from the grand piano, glockenspiel, bass guitar, double speed guitar, mandolin, Spanish and acoustic guitar through to, of course, tubular bells.

Some critics feel that this record epitomises progressive music's excessive nature, in all its technological glory. In complete disregard for the opinions of experts, music fans continue to highly rate Oldfield's debut as an ambient masterpiece. It was, however, very much a concept of its era. To think of anyone making 25 minutes tracks like these ten years, or even five years, later would have been laughable. As is so often the case, it was about being in the right place, at the right time. For Oldfield, that meant Britain, 1972/73.

Nothing stereotypes progressive music quite like ***Tubular Bells*** with its two meandering tracks. With no lyrics, it was left for the music to cover a wide spectrum of emotions, ranging from joyous to morose. It began with the sound of a haunting piano then, seconds later, the menacing presence of an electric organ took the lead. The notes were repeated around two bars, making a ghostly, hypnotic impact. Gradually additional instruments joined in, bass, flute, electric guitar, speed guitar... The building blocks continually expanded, with occasional bouts of explosions and implosions, and without warning reduce from ecstatic pleasure to lonesome reflection. During the course of 49 minutes the arrangements weaved instruments together as though a musical tapestry, wandering from piano, bass, guitars, glockenspiels, Spanish guitar and so forth.

It conjured thoughts of an eventful journey and, at times, a manic-depressive syndrome, with wildly conflicting moods placed adjacent to each other. No better was this illustrated than on the closing sequence. For several minutes it gave an impression that **Tubular Bells** would be brought slowly to a mournful close. It was like being sat down in church, attending a funeral. The atmosphere was sombre, contemplative. Then, just when it seemed it was all over, along came one final piece (the Sailor's hornpipe segment) lasting barely a minute. As abruptly as it began the delirious jig was over and so too Oldfield's first offering.

Somewhat quaintly, the original LP sleeve quoted a reference to Glorious Stereophonic Sound - as if a new discovery had been made. There was also another joke on the cover that you had to be there, in 1973, to understand. 'This stereo record cannot be played on old tin boxes no matter what they are fitted with. If you are in possession of such equipment please hand it into the nearest police station'.

(41)

DOOLITTLE – PIXIES (1989)

(Debaser/Tame/Wave Of Mutilation/I Bleed/Here Comes Your Man/Dead/Monkey Gone To Heaven/Mr Grieves/ Crackity Jones/La La Love You/No 13 Baby/There Goes My Gun/Hey/Silver/Gouge Away)

Top Track: Debaser

Memphis, Nashville, Detroit, Liverpool, London, New York, San Francisco and L.A., all at one point, critical venues in rock and dance development. Who could have predicted that to this elite list would be added Seattle, giving birth to a volatile form of rock towards the end of the eighties? Grunge displayed vulture traits, by way of siphoning Punk's minimalism and pulverising it head-first into Heavy Metal's deep bass thuds. Such wildly polarised subgenres being welded together made for an improbable, and yet highly workable, alliance. Enigmatically, one of the early frontrunners in the Grunge movement originated from Boston, Massachusetts, several hundred miles away from the epicentre – the Pixies.

Their breakthrough occurred upon signing to UK label 4.A.D and the release of their second album, **Doolittle**. *Debaser* exemplified Grunge's excitable obsession with manic momentum, extreme alterations in musical tones and piercing lead vocals. The lyrics became almost secondary to the angry rock emanating from punishing guitar riffs and throbbing bass licks. The words didn't make for pretty reading, with references to blood and a dead heart on (*Dead*), whilst in the true tradition of hardcore Punk virtually the only lyric to *There Goes My Gun* was the song's title. Elsewhere it didn't get any friendlier, on *Wave Of Mutilation* a car was driven into the ocean and on *I Bleed* vampires had a feast.

One of the key tracks, *Monkey Gone To Heaven*, gave an explanation for the bizarre album cover featuring a monkey surrounded by the numbers 5, 6 and 7. The lyrics were seemingly beyond comprehension, with some kind of numbering connection being made with man (5), the devil (6) and God (7). There was quaint rhyming going on for sure but what was it about? With greater observation of the give-away clues referring to a hole in the sky it became apparent that environmental concerns were uppermost. Lead singer, Frank Black, would also subsequently clarify the numbering sequence had been taken from Hebrew numerology.

The words appearing on ***Doolittle*** were psychopathic, frightening, often seriously disturbing, but from *Debaser* through to *Gouge Away*, the experience was total roller-coaster exhilaration. The Pixies successfully absorbed core Grunge ingredients producing a blueprint few could imitate. They should have been as famous as Nirvana.

(42)

MARQUEE MOON – TELEVISION (1977)

(***See No Evil/Venus/Friction/Marquee Moon/Elevation/ Guiding Light/Prove It/Torn Curtain***)

Top Track: Marquee Moon

In the UK, Punk was welcomed as a Year Zero revolution. America, however, appeared unwilling to subscribe to an elementary re-writing of the history textbooks. For rock fans in the US, lately milked on a highly-saturated diet of AOR, excellent musicianship and lyrical thoughtfulness were still viewed as integral components in their listening pleasure. Their reaction against conservative/ dinosaur bands adhered to a more refined path than heard in Britain, with the mainstream eager to encourage reconciliation, rather than division, with the past.

Stemming from the CBGB scene in New York (alongside Patti Smith, Blondie, the Ramones and Talking Heads) Television personified US New Wave (a safe-for-radio, commercially marketable diversification of Punk). They took their cue from the late-sixties (Quicksilver Messenger Service, Love, Buffalo

Springfield and, unavoidably, the Velvet Underground), with much of their debut, **Marquee Moon**, strongly influenced by twin-guitar techniques from that decade.

The title-track magnificently showed-off their capabilities, with an epic ten minutes dual between Tom Verlaine and Richard Lloyd. It was a glorious tour-de-force that veered away from the noise thrashes associated with Punk. The single *Prove It* b/w *Venus* became an instant classic, ironically receiving greatest acknowledgement in the UK, where a rave review of the album in New Musical Express brought Television to the attention of an appreciative audience. Once again, a US talent turned to Britain for acceptance, where **Marquee Moon** was seen as a New Wave masterpiece, pleasing Year Zero believers and those old enough to remember life before Punk.

Unfortunately, this wasn't the beginning of a long and illustrious career. A follow-up two years later failed to maintain the standards set on their astonishing debut, an essential addition to any respectable collection. In 2003 N.M.E. rated it the fourth best album of all-time – high praise indeed, and showing that after over 25 years it remains one of the shining lights from the late-seventies.

(43)

<u>IN UTERO – NIRVANA (1993)</u>

(Serve The Servants/Scentless Apprentice/Heart-Shaped Box/Rape Me/Frances Farmer Will Have Her Revenge On Seattle/Dumb/Very Ape/Milk It/Pennyroyal Tea/Radio Friendly Unit Shifter/Tourette's/All Apologies)

Top Track: Scentless Apprentice

Although DGC (David Geffen Company) anticipated cash registers ringing when Nirvana began work on the follow-up to **Nevermind**, the album's architect, Kurt Cobain, had other ideas. Steve Albini, renowned for his microphone-placement in the studio methodology as a producer/engineer, was given the task of overseeing the recording sessions. On realising the band's choice and, even more so, on hearing the first results of their latest efforts, there was dismay at Geffen. Far from being another money-spinning giant to bolster the corporate profits, Nirvana seemed determined on committing commercial suicide. Where were the harmonious characteristics enshrined on **Nevermind** and where were the tunes? The band held their nerve, with Cobain claiming that the new album was more akin to what he, as a music fan, would prefer to own.

In Utero (the original title I Hate Myself And Want To Die was more accurate) began not with a new *Smells Like Teen Spirit* but a dense, sludge-laden stab at several annoyances in Cobain's life (notably difficult relationships with the media). *Serve The Servants* was lyrically uncompromising, bordering on ultra-depressing, but decisively directing towards the rest of the album's true Grunge credentials. Next was the screaming/shouting saga that went by the name *Scentless Apprentice*. Cobain's hollering vocals were capable of shattering windows within a mile radius - it felt like a man in dire straits, struggling to come to terms with his own twisted fate. The most controversial cut, *Rape Me*, received strong criticism, clearly not understood by those who probably hadn't even listened to it - it was actually an anti-rape anthem! Of the tracks on **In Utero** it was the closest in attitude to the imposing, monstrous beast it followed, with the intro similar to that on *Smells Like Teen Spirit*.

A popular Grunge trend was using one-word song titles but, as if to emphasise they were different from the rest, Nirvana came out with the elongated *Frances Farmer Will Have Her Revenge On Seattle*. Its quiet passages were intermittently torpedoed by loud sonic explosions (see also *Pennyroyal Tea*), only to resume with gentleness – unsettling and strangely captivating. *Radio Friendly Unit Shifter* (this set had anything but 'multi-million seller' stamped on it) growled an aggressive course, contributing to the album's overall, but unjust, perception as a poor follow-up.

In a peculiar sense, Cobain made a record that he was happy with, for it owed more to their debut, **Bleach**, with its frenzied Punk mayhem. The record company was unimpressed and the teenagers milked on **Nevermind** were bewildered, but the open-minded appreciated **In Utero** for its pure honesty. It captures a man on the brink.

(44)

UNKNOWN PLEASURES – JOY DIVISION (1979)

(*Disorder/Day Of The Lords/Candidate/Insight/New Dawn Fades/She's Lost Control/ Shadowplay/ Wilderness / Interzone/I Remember Nothing*)

Top Track: Disorder

Britain in May 1979 saw a new administration, with a Conservative Government elected on a promise of change. Regardless of her pledges outside Downing Street, the UK under Margaret Thatcher's premiership would be anything but united. For the scores disadvantaged as a result of the new regime's policies – specifically the poor, unemployed and homeless – Joy Division became a mouthpiece, rising to prominence with harrowing songs engulfed by alienation and profound hopelessness.

Unknown Pleasures was visibly the work of individuals whose introspective thoughts were obtained from the cold, wet and dreariness of modern urban life in Britain. Songs that in rock's tomorrows were accredited classic status could be found here in abundance. *Shadowplay* featured lyrics drawing attention to suicide that subsequently (as with many Joy Division tracks) became a source of curious interest to clue-searchers, trying to unscramble the tragedy befalling the band in May 1980.

Apathy and despondency were the dominating emotions on the eerie *New Dawn Fades* as Ian Curtis contemplated a sense of directionless lifestyle. Whilst much of the set wallowed on cosmopolitan issues, on *She's Lost Control* personal crisis played central role. Curtis suffered from epilepsy and, in confessional mood, poured out fearful apprehension. The superbly titled *Disorder* (here was a track pointing towards later directions circa New Order) and the anthem stature of *Day Of The Lords* stood out as key moments. On *Insight* the tormented lead singer unconvincingly suggested he was no longer afraid but, oh if only the truth were known. Check out also, the straight-ahead Punk blast heard on *Interzone*!

Some called Joy Division's music barren, stark, depressing. It was often categorised as industrialised rock (somewhat stretching the definition), sometimes post-Punk but whichever way, **Unknown Pleasures** achieved a legacy that reverberated throughout the following years. This and **Closer** are amongst the best work recorded by a British band, the real sadness being that it had to end so disastrously.

(45)

THE STONE ROSES (1989)

(I Wanna Be Adored/She Bangs The Drums/ Waterfall/Don't Stop/Bye Bye Badman/Elizabeth My Dear/(Song For My) Sugar Spun Sister/Made Of Stone/ Shoot You Down/This Is The One/I Am The Resurrection)

Top Track: I Am The Resurrection

After twenty years spearheading popular music, Britain suffered a hiatus during the eighties. Classic UK albums from this era were rare and even more difficult was pinpointing the reason for this sharp decline. You could blame it on a preoccupation with videos in response to the launch of MTV (the popularity of new romantics on this channel didn't help matters). Maybe it was the advent of the Compact Disc, whereby crystal purity replaced innovation. Perhaps it was Punk's short-lived attempt to destroy the dinosaurs, but there was no avoiding a dismal reflection that the eighties had been disappointing. For guitar bands especially it was a period to forget. As dusk began to settle on the decade a band from Manchester released their debut album, with few at that time appreciating the enormity of its importance.

By the late-eighties popular music tastes in Britain were severed into two rigidly defined, directionless, camps - rock (pretty much the die-hards from NWOBHM) versus dance. **The Stone Roses** embraced the best elements from both, with an emphasis also placed on reincarnating US/UK pop from the glory days. They took in narrowly separated influences from the mid-sixties, such as the jingle-jangle feel-good factor by the Byrds and simply great melodic tunes as immortalised by the Beatles. By adding a contemporary dance rhythm they unwittingly tapped into a golden formula. Electric guitars and groovy dance music under the same roof, how good could it get?

As if to reinforce the message, they announced their arrival with unrestrained confidence with lead singer, Ian Brown, declaring intent right from the off, *I Wanna Be Adored*. The tunes rolled with continuity as *She Bangs The Drums* and the glorious air-guitar splendour of *Waterfall* increased the adrenalin buzz. Meanwhile, *Don't Stop* succeeded in fusing a heavy-rock texture with loaded swirling feedback and slurred vocals. The acutely sixties-flavoured *Bye Bye Badman* came across as a strange brew, grasping ingredients from bands associated with the Brit Invasion, notably the Dave Clark Five and the Hollies - wonderfully invigorating, a pre-Brit Pop great.

The Stone Roses systematically 'reinvented' the electric guitar, its eleven songs celebrating the pleasures of six-strings. For sheer joyous rock, few songs have bettered *This Is The One, Made Of Stone* and *Shoot You Down*, whilst the lengthy *I Am The Resurrection* showcased John Squire's virtuosity with the frets. They were leaving themselves open to accusations of conceitedness but, in hindsight, they really were the resurrection, British rock's saviours. It's a cliché, but this album's significance is of biblical proportions.

(46)

IS THIS IT – THE STROKES (2001)

(*Is This It/The Modern Age/Soma/Barely Legal/ Someday/Alone, Together/Last Nite/Hard To Explain/ New York City Cops/Trying Your Luck/Take It Or Leave It*)

Top Track: *The Modern Age*

The first official release from the Strokes, *The Modern Age EP* (*The Modern Age*, *Last Nite* and *Barely Legal*), instigated the rebirth of garage rock. These songs, recorded in unconventional settings, were viewed as revolutionary by some, reactionary by others but either way, word of mouth recommendation quickly spread. In just a few weeks they were preoccupying the minds of discerning rock music fans, starving for something that excited. Revered as the greatest band in a generation, their debut album was greeted with huge expectations. **Is This It** justified the hype.

It amounted to eleven tracks stripped of unnecessary intricacies that blatantly revealed traces of US New Wave and the Velvet Underground (*The Modern Age* had striking similarities with the VU's *I'm Waiting For The Man*). Influences at times were far too obvious, *Trying Your Luck*, *Take It Or Leave It* and *Alone, Together* had a lust for unsung heroes, Television, whilst beneath the surface lurked memories of the New York Dolls and Talking Heads. Horrific events on September 11th resulted in *New York City Cops* being withdrawn from US copies. It was understandable, given its critical comments but musically here was one of the highlights. Trampling on the burial grounds of garage land, *Soma*, *Last Nite* and *Hard To Explain* brought those 1976 New Wave days flooding back.

Distracting controversy came by way of the album's front cover featuring a hand on naked hip but was it male or female? Did it really matter? Seemingly so, for a while there was a serious possibility that high street retailers weren't going to stock the record in its original sleeve. Fears were raised that innocent young eyes would be corrupted by the sight of one glove, one hand and the offending nakedness (that actually showed nothing). Fortunately, censorship didn't reach new levels of stupidity with *Is This It*, cover as well, gracing the shelves of all good stores everywhere. If anything, more offence was found inside the cover, where gruesome mug shots of the band members, manager, producer and 'guru' awaited - what weird hairstyles!

In much the same way that Oasis brought nothing new to rock's table, the Strokes could hardly be described as pioneers. However, by 2001 originality was no longer a crucial aspect within an artist's arsenal. The thing that really counted was composing songs that interested and enriched, regardless of whether ideas were taken from someone else's creation. In these modern times people don't always have the necessary luxury to allow a collection of songs to 'grow' on them. Music, therefore, must make an immediate impact, by-passing the brain and reaching straight for the heart. *Is This It* did exactly that.

(47)

THE SMITHS (1984)

(Reel Around The Fountain/You've Got Everything Now/ Miserable Lie/Pretty Girls Make Graves/The Hand That Rocks The Cradle/This Charming Man/Still Ill/Hand In Glove/What Difference Does It Make?/I Don't Owe You Anything/Suffer Little Children)
Top Track: What Difference Does It Make?

Quality British music disappeared on a sabbatical during the early-eighties. This lean period, beginning in the aftermath of post-Punk, showed few signs of abating as a further poor harvest ensued during early 1984. The debut release by the Smiths presented the first sprinkling of hope that change was in the air.

Consisting of singer (Morrissey, or 'voice' as he was credited on the LP), drummer (Mike Joyce), bass player (Andy Rourke) and an imaginative electric guitarist, Johnny Marr, the four-piece traditional rock line-up looked to be staging a comeback. Refreshingly, with new romanticism still reverberating, there wasn't a synthesiser or big disco beat audible anywhere on ***The Smiths***. Equally, there were no thrills or garish production blurring Northern grit realism.

Miles from the glitzy, party-time music paraded by recent UK acts such as Human League, Depeche Mode and Culture Club the band's dark lyrics dug downwards into controversial and miserable realms. *The Hand That Rocks The Cradle* and, in particular, *Reel Around The Fountain* caused speculation in the national press of a questionable paedophile interest. Immense unease was also levied at *Suffer Little Children*, analytically probing the infamous Moors Murders.

If clues were needed as to what or who inspired the Smiths to pen such wretched verses, they surely rested somewhere in the sixties. They were not, however, the happy days of mini-skirts and moon landings but chilling evil as symbolised by Brady and Hindley. The musical inheritance that they embellished owed as much to the Byrds (noted especially on *The Hand That Rocks The Cradle*) as it did recent mentors Joy Division (listen to the deadened drumming on *Still Ill* and *Hand In Glove*).

For a 45 minutes exercise in plunging macabre depths, they set new grim standards. Apathy (can't be bothered to get a job on *You've Got Everything Now*), warped humour (falling out of bed during a dream on *Reel Around The Fountain*) and monstrous horror (digging a shallow grave on *Suffer Little Children*) were emotional extremities rare in a UK album. ***Meat Is Murder*** (1985) and ***The Queen Is Dead*** (1986) are also recommended but their debut caps them all due to its lasting resonance.

(48)

OK COMPUTER – RADIOHEAD (1997)

(*Airbag/Paranoid Android/Subterranean Homesick Alien/ Exit Music (For A Film)/Let Down/Karma Police/Fitter Happier/Electioneering/Climbing Up The Walls/No Surprises/Lucky/The Tourist*)

Top Track: Paranoid Android

This was a 'concept' album for a new generation of progressive rock fans and insomniacs plagued by pre-millennium tension. If critics were to also be believed, **OK Computer** was not only the perfect soundtrack to close the 20th Century, it was an equal to the legendary records by the Beatles and Dylan.

Detouring around the obvious option of duplicating *The Bends*, Radiohead swerved off the safe road and into the unknown. *Airbag*, swamped by claustrophobic guitar-noises meandered through a wayward adventure, with life's uncertainties and anxieties hidden amongst bizarre lyrics. It acted as a complementary precursor for *Paranoid Android*, a pin-balling mesh of acoustic guitars and unpredictable, electrifying explosions. *Subterranean Homesick Alien* featured escapist, almost suicidal lyrics, with the subdued arrangements exaggerating the gloom. Telling of aliens hovering overhead set to Pink Floyd styled atmospherics, the screwed-up narrator yearned for nothing more than to be captured and taken away in a U.F.O. – with the old millennium fast drawing to an end, it seemed that escape remained the only frontier not fully explored.

Exit Music (For A Film) was sufficiently morbid to make even the happiest soul consider jumping from the bridge – it just felt so discouraging, so empty. *Let Down* temporarily raised spirits, only for the paranoid panorama to resume with further spells of mental chaos on *Karma Police*. *Fitter Happier* was dispensable nonsense... *Electioneering* was painful on the ears... *Climbing Up The Walls* (an apt alternative album title if ever there was!) harnessed a diverse range of guitars, thumping drumbeats and Thom Yorke's vocals sounding as though recorded in a smashed-up phone box. It fell on *No Surprises* to provide light relief from overwhelming darkness. However, by studying the lyrics it was soon apparent that this was no happy occasion either.

The band may deny a concept, but there certainly was a continuity (revolving around madness and modern materialism) loosely connecting the songs. Greatest albums polls produced not long after its release placed it in some very lofty positions. One UK monthly magazine reflecting the views of its readers rated it at Number 1. Yes, it's good but for most serious rock history students that surely was going too far in applause. **The Bends** is better.

(49)

MOONDANCE – VAN MORRISON (1970)

(*And It Stoned Me/Moondance/Crazy Love/Caravan/Into The Mystic/Come Running/These Dreams Of You/Brand New Day/Everyone/Glad Tidings*)

Top Track: Into The Mystic

The Belfast mystic rethought his plans after the critical acclaim that greeted **Astral Weeks** in 1968 failed to convert in to sizeable sales. Worshippers of his hypnotic work, anticipating a continuation from where the bluesy/folk *Slim Slow Slider* left off, were in for a disappointment. The broad-minded, willing to listen to something that didn't retrace the same trodden steps, were in for a treat.

Released in February 1970, **Moondance** captures Morrison at a new decade's dawn, re-discovering his love for US Soul. Whereas its predecessor stoically avoided mainstream approval, the new album overflowed with short, extremely commercialised material. There were many options for a 45 but, although not being an obvious front-runner, the honour was given to *Come Running*. It was, by his recent chart standards, an unmitigated success reaching the US Top 40, his highest placing since *Brown Eyed Girl*.

And It Stoned Me fondly recalled fanciful days of youth, two boys enjoying the simple things in life - fishing, listening to transistor radios and generally getting wet. To a backdrop of horns and a swaggering ambience, it set the easy-going nature for the on-coming rapturous parade of blue-eyed Soul. Thoughts of innocent pleasures were dismissed on *Moondance* as Morrison made clear his evening intentions centred on romantic fun outside, under the moon - a song full of raunchiness accompanied by pastiche Jazz. The seductive theme continued on the delectable *Crazy Love* before **Moondance** progressed onwards to two monumental Morrison tracks.

Caravan and *Into The Mystic* rate amongst his very best, with the latter coming closest to the enchanting dreaminess heard on **Astral Weeks**. One of rock's finest 3:25 minutes began so sweetly, strings hung in suspended animation, layered by Morrison's honey-textured vocals. His words depicted an idealistic vision but, 'heavy-meaningful' hippy wisdom asides the song's instrumentation delicately carried a beautiful message. Turn the lights out, lay flat on the floor, breathe in, breathe out and relax.

Side 1 always receives the popular and critical attention. It needs reminding that Side 2 matched the strong opening sequence, with *Come Running*, *Brand New Day* and *Glad Tidings* worthy of high ranking alongside the all-time best Morrison songs. **Astral Weeks** takes time before its magical qualities brighten your life. **Moondance** hits the mark first time.

(50)

<u>NEON BIBLE – ARCADE FIRE (2007)</u>

(Black Mirror/Keep The Car Running/Neon Bible/ Intervention/Black Wave/Bad Vibrations/Ocean Of Noise/ The Well And The Lighthouse/(Antichrist Television Blues)/Windowsill/No Cars Go/ My Body Is A Cage)

Top Track: Intervention

A former Quebec church/cafe, converted in to a studio, was the unlikely setting for one of the new millennium's greatest albums, so far. Such an audacious environment explained why **Neon Bible** had an echoing, at times spooky, spacious atmosphere. That haunting sensation was continually reflected from the songs, many of which also beamed with the presence of influential spirits.

Black Mirror felt as though the Velvet Underground had gate-crashed the congregation, but historic bohemian rockers were not Arcade Fire's main inspiration source. A quest for divine guidance prospered very early, but brought into question God's commitment on *Neon Bible* – a weird folksy tune, fuelled by a sense of ominous foreboding. As if to press the point home religious violation, perhaps sacrilege, occurred when the 'church' dwelling musicians started using the 'resident' organ on *Intervention*. This track provoked debate regarding its meaning, for was it about death or the Iraq War/Intervention/Liberation? It's best to forget the political controversies and instead, enjoy the delights that sparkle – church organ and Pop in perfect harmony, like never before.

Black Wave/Bad Vibrations span creepiness off into other worlds, two songs bolted together in an unfathomable marriage – the first half gothic ghosts, the second conquered by demonic possession. Biblical references were also scattered throughout *The Well And The*

Lighthouse, however, this high-flying stunner called upon more earthly assistance, in the form of the VU and synthesiser masters circa New Order, to find its grounding.

Further probing troubled faith came forward on *(Antichrist Television Blues)*, a blistering acoustic tune with singer, Win Butler, asking searching questions of God's plans. More uncertainties ensued, a desperate drive out into the darkness, only to conclude with sorrowful self-realisation. The church organ was put to further effective use on *My Body Is A Cage*, a brooding lament on self-doubt and disturbed thoughts.

Rarely has an album been so overwhelming in a search for redemption, a need for promise fulfilled. Rarer too, has it been dutifully delivered with so much intense passion and extraordinary musical variance, engulfing darkness and light.

(51)

LIEGE AND LIEF – FAIRPORT CONVENTION (1969)

(Come All Ye/Reynardine/Matty Groves/Farewell, Farewell/ The Deserter/Medley (The Lark In The Morning/Rakish Paddy/Fox-Hunter's Jig/Toss The Feathers)/Tam Lin/ Crazy Man Michael)

Top Track: *Farewell, Farewell*

There are few disputes that their fourth LP remains the most important English Folk album. Recorded during the summer of '69, just weeks after their drummer, Martin Lamble, was killed in a road traffic accident, **Liege And Lief** far from being mournful, shined like a sunny day. To say it warrants popular and critical recognition as a crucial landmark in British music is an understatement.

At a time when UK and US contemporary tastes were becoming obsessed with heavy, metallic rock, Fairport Convention pursued their own goals. Not for them, wildly explosive electric guitar solos but instead, a devoted love for traditional Folk given a modern facelift. This album's strength lay in the stunning depth of musicianship, aligned with some truly inspired song selections. The band (at least on this occasion) consisted of Ashley Hutchings (bass), Dave Mattacks (drums), Simon Nicol (guitar/vocals), Dave Swarbrick (violin/viola/fiddle), Richard Thompson (guitar/vocals) and Sandy Denny (arguably, England's finest female Folk singer). It was a line-up that collectively far outweighed the individual parts.

Come All Ye produced a lively, jovial ambience, in part autobiographical – an undiluted celebration of joyous music. The band extended an invitation to all and sundry, as they played the fiddle, violin, drum, guitar and bass, whilst all along it was Denny's adorable vocals that roused the earth's spirit. It came complete with an infectious chorus guaranteed to get the audience joining in. *Matty Groves*, lasting over eight minutes, narrated adulterous woes and deceit, with the 'wicked' lovers in question both ending up on the wrong side of Lord Darnell's sword. Meanwhile, *Crazy Man Michael* relayed the tale of the wandering madman who spent his time talking to the night and day, whilst *Tam Lin* gave dire warnings about going to Carter Hall.

The strange thing was that although recorded in the 20th Century, it echoed England's wealthy Folk music history spanning five hundred years (the majority of the songs were traditional compositions, re-arranged for a new perspective). Listen to the fabulous instrumental *Medley* and the tearful ballad *Farewell, Farewell* and allow yourself to travel back in time. Leave the hustle and bustle of today's fast-moving lifestyle, just for 40 minutes, and submerge in to an alternative world where the pace is slower and colourful characters await. Watch out for the angry Lord Darnell and keep away from mad Michael. **Liege And Lief** is akin to the early albums by the Band in their warming respects for a bygone era.

(52)

SWORDFISHTROMBONES – TOM WAITS (1983)

(*Underground/Shore Leave/Dave Butcher/Johnsburg, Illinois/16 Shells From A Thirty-Ought-Six/Town With No Cheer/In The Neighborhood/Just Another Sucker On The Vine/Frank's Wild Years/Swordfishtrombone/Down, Down, Down/Soldier's Things/Gin Soaked Boy/Trouble's Braids/ Rainbirds*)

Top Track: Shore Leave

Tom Waits sang, shouted and growled his way through an eclectic set, at times slowing down to lethargic pace, talking rather than singing, whispering instead of hollering. Miles from the surface populated by AOR and New Romanticism he rambled deep into subterranean murkiness, unearthing intermittent elements of film-score (the narrative *Shore Leave*), smoky bar-room Blues (*Frank's Wild Years* and *Johnsburg, Illinois*), whilst the irritating gruffness on *In The Neighborhood* had to be heard to be believed. The opening track's pivotal line referring to a world going on underground was totally appropriate for the album as a whole.

Some tracks were short, feeling like nothing more than half-completed sketches (eight were less than 2:30 minutes with *Trouble's Braids* registering at just 1:18 minutes). It made for a free-flowing, anarchical mix punctuated by varying emotions swinging at whim from assertive bellowing on *Down, Down, Down* and *16 Shells From A Thirty-Ought-Six* to subdued resignation via a ballad, *Soldier's Things*. All in all, it was confirmation that bohemian music needn't result in a sprawling mess of contrived nonsense.

It sounded like nothing else from 1983 or, for that matter, the decade. For this reason it doesn't suffer from the hallmarks associated with most releases from the eighties, standing high on merit as a charming, individualistic performance by a talent unjustly underrated. In searching for Tom Waits at his best it always comes back to ***Swordfishtrombones***.

(53)

TOGETHER ALONE – CROWDED HOUSE (1993)

(***Kare Kare/In My Command/Nails In My Feet/Black & White Boy/Fingers Of Love/Pineapple Head/Locked Out/ Private Universe/Walking On The Spot/Distant Sun/ Catherine Wheels/Skin Feeling/Together Alone***)

Top Track: Private Universe

With a change in producer, Youth, and a different recording studio (Kare Kare near Auckland, New Zealand), Crowded House set about expanding their sound. Just one listen to the finished product shows that those aspirations were fully achieved. Whereas ***Woodface*** travelled down a pop-flavoured path, ***Together Alone*** combined styles as varied as rock, folk, new wave, gospel and traditional Maori rhythms.

On previous albums they generally separated the two primary strands to their musical chemistry, namely soft rock and heavenly acoustic tunes. The razor-sharp *In My Command* attacked this firm division, with a glorious shot of power-chord heaviness (reminiscent of the Beatles circa '65) blasting towards a fabulous sing-along chorus line. *Skin Feeling* repeated this forcefulness but there was one simple rule that defined Crowded House (or specifically, the band's main songwriter and chief architect, Neil Finn) – make sure that the tunes are memorable. The Beatles were always a strong influence but, in many respects, the songs here absorbed ideas from thirty years of popular music (*Private Universe* was a tune Simon and Garfunkel could have benefited from, *Locked Out* took a prompt from the late-seventies Punk/New Wave era, whilst *Kare Kare* had similarities with mid-eighties Dire Straits).

Crowded House's true colours were evident in Finn's skill at connecting South Pacific charm, performed by the Te Waka Huia Cultural Group Choir, with modern Pop. *Catherine Wheels*, for example, concluded with an enchanting, hip-swaying tinge that beautifully captured New Zealand's multi-cultural, cheek-by-jowl society. Similarly, the title-track went where few records had dared go before, by fusing a rustic brass band with Maori harmonies. On paper it was an awkward concept but, with crafted production they moulded a unique Polynesian sound. From *Kare Kare* through to the indigenous drumbeats signing-off *Together Alone*, this album weaved together numerous genres, creating wide-ranging textures. In essence, it symbolised the peaceful co-existence of different races in NZ, post 1872.

Together Alone received widespread critical acclaim (and many ***** reviews) but couldn't build on the popularity of its predecessor. The band's adventurous excursion, wandering from Punk pastiche, through acoustic arrangements, piano-based structures (*Walking On The Spot* was delightful) and Maori spirits, failed to excite an audience that preferred continuations of *Weather With You*. The intrigued, wanting to know where to start their Crowded House collection, are recommended to begin here. Put the CD on, close your eyes, you could almost be Down Under.

(54)

RADIO CITY – BIG STAR (1974)

(*O My Soul/Life Is White/Way Out West/What's Goin' Ahn/You Get What You Deserve/Mod Lang/Back Of A Car/Daisy Glaze/ She's A Mover/September Gurls/Morpha Too/I'm In Love With A Girl*)

Top Track: O My Soul

Whilst American music during the early-seventies struggled to find a new unifying force, Big Star (fronted by former lead singer with the Box Tops, Alex Chilton) preferred to look over their shoulders to the previous decade, nostalgically to key acts from the US West Coast and the Brit Invasion. Using harmonies borrowed from the Beatles, Kinks, Beach Boys, Byrds and Moby Grape, the band's debut LP, **#1 Record**, fused many aspects of sixties pop, folk and soul. Sandwiched in between *Feel* and *St 100/6* lay musical perfection in tracks such as *The Ballad Of El Goodo, Don't Lie To Me, When My Baby's Beside Me, Try Again* and a stunning ode to young love, *Thirteen*.

On **Radio City** they persisted with ignoring the growing US trend for searching out new genres, once again excavating the sixties grave. The repeat prescription paid good dividends with twelve songs that embraced the golden decade's high-points. Rock seldom felt so cool (*Back Of A Car, Way Out West* and *You Get What You Deserve*), nor so innocently simplistic (the 1:48 minutes *I'm In Love With A Girl*). Chilton's vocals were characteristically strained by a vulnerable tension, the band's accompaniment often underwhelming, but with so many effervescent tunes **Radio City** was a first-class lesson in 'power-pop' sixties revivalism.

Their most famous song is housed here, but Big Star's appeal went much further than a sugar-sweetened cover version of *September Gurls*. Often a true classic doesn't start receiving such a tag until several years after its release. Generally over-looked by record buyers (1974 was a funny old year) it seemed that only credible critics latched on to its wondrous stories. By the eighties this began to change, with a new generation of bands (R.E.M, Teenage Fanclub and the Replacements) quoting Big Star as a major inspiration. Listening to this record, it does tantalisingly feel that maybe, just maybe, if the Beatles had re-formed, they may have sounded something like this.

(55)

METALLICA (1991)

(Enter Sandman/Sad But True/Holier Than Thou/The Unforgiven/Wherever I May Roam/Don't Tread On Me/ Through The Never/Nothing Else Matters/Of Wolf And Man/The God That Failed/My Friend Of Misery/The Struggle Within)

Top Track: Enter Sandman

In the year that Grunge went overground the final nail in the Heavy Metal coffin was hammered in. Decisive signs were heard during 1991 that symbolically signalled the end of rock's wildly erratic animal. Nirvana's cheerleading anthems played a significant part in this downfall, but few anticipated an enemy from within.

There were not many doubters that some aspects of rock were generally falling into the wrong hands and that the new 'heroes' of the genre did not pay the same respects as the pioneers. Formerly the bastion of sincere bands with designs on taking the electric guitar to unexplored limits, the eighties witnessed a dramatic decline in creative fortunes. Metallica were renowned for being the upholders of rock's latest hard spirit, with a series of highly-rated thrash based albums. Their 5th release destroyed all of this, in the process re-setting the margins that defined a great rock record.

Metallica gave few initial clues that it was a landmark moment. Indeed, the dark sleeve cover (resulting in the alternative title, The Black Album) suggested it was business as usual. One listen to it, however, was all it took to appreciate that rock had approached a new dawn. *Enter Sandman* began unassumingly, a delicate introduction, then lightning cracked and thunder clapped, a storm force gale roared in. There was an immediate sense that rock's comfortably numb status quo was about to suffer structural damage. It was a song to rattle the strongest-willed, powered by stupendous riffs and pounding drumbeats – even the lyrics portrayed the onset of darkness. It felt like a troublesome calling-card intended for scores of HM bands. Metallica's new simple, hard-driven formulas were devoid of unwanted intricacies, and with one master stroke they abolished the ridiculous pretence ruining rock of late. In its place they left behind a stripped to basics model that effectively killed HM.

Pastoral flavourings and slow compositions were not normally within scope on their albums but they not only ripped-up the form book, they also reinstated a forgotten concept – tunes. Coming straight after the full-throttle *Holier Than Thou*, the next big surprise was *The Unforgiven* with thoughtfully arranged stringed instrumentation, bells and a melody. If that wasn't shocking enough, a further 'ballad' followed later with *Nothing Else Matters* (the chances are that by now the traditionalists had jumped ship). The old school gained some comfort through familiar surroundings in tracks such as *Don't Tread On Me*, *Through The Never*, *Of Wolf And Man* and the mammoth *The Struggle Within*.

Gone were the brain-spinning, bone-crunching 'noises' of eighties HM, possessed by Satanic lyrics and an unhealthy obsession with fables glorifying gruesome gore and death. A new order in rock emerged, founded on a desire to re-establish integrity. In the aftermath of this massive album much soul-searching occurred in the land frequented by longhaired heavies. Old enemies continued the fight against everything that Metallica now epitomised, whilst thrash-metal enthusiasts accused them of a Judas scale betrayal but one thing was for sure – a long overdue debate had begun, resulting in an extraordinary splintering within the rock genre.

(56)

AUTOBAHN – KRAFTWERK (1974)

(Autobahn/Kometenmelodie 1/Kometenmelodie 2/ Mitternacht/Morgenspaziergang)

Top Track: *Autobahn*

How many albums do most people have by German bands? A small handful maybe, invariably by progressive synthesiser-orientated outfits from the seventies (Can and Tangerine Dream), but even many respectable collections often have nothing originating from Germany. During 1974 one German band, with an innovative vision on populist culture, patronisingly labelled by the media as Kraut rock, captured global imaginations. Patriotically, their hit 45 was also sung in their native language, a track that gave its title to their breakthrough album.

Making a record about a long, tedious stretch of road doesn't spring to mind as being a good idea for a groundbreaker. Furthermore, creating a track that spanned an entire side of vinyl was in itself a daunting task. Forget the edited 45 snippet of *Autobahn*, to do justice the lively pleasure that is the epic 22:42 minutes version must be heard. Surely the best song ever for driving in a car, Kraftwerk simulated the experience of lengthy automobile journeys, from tooting horns, dreary straight lines to fast-flowing fun drives. That it proved so successful was all the more surprising given the times in which it was created. Even by 1974 synthesisers were still eyed with suspicion by traditional musicians. Queen, for example, specifically went to lengths on their LP covers to distance themselves from the controversial instrument, using the comment – No Synthesisers!

Despite being expansive *Autobahn* featured few words but, even with a language barrier, they were irresistibly infectious. In any case, did the lyrics make sense to anyone outside Germany? They were available on the back cover to the LP, not that this 'helpful' inclusion made it any easier to decipher what they were about. Ultimately, it didn't depend on understandable words to get its message across which, whilst not immediately obvious, was simple enough – this was the sound of the future. Comparisons were made with *Fun Fun Fun*, given that fahr'n, fahr'n fahr'n sounded similar and Kraftwerk sang in a manner resembling the Beach Boys. Both tracks also had cars as the central theme but, in all other respects, the two couldn't have been more different. The Beach Boys belonged to a former era, Kraftwerk were making music coming from our tomorrows.

They were instrumental in formulating a style, possibly a genre, which would dominate the UK Pop scene in the early-eighties, hugely influential on the Human League, Depeche Mode and Yazoo. With the ushering in of New Romantics during 1980-1 Kraftwerk's Electronica reached out to the popular masses. Fittingly, they scored a belated UK Number 1 in 1982 with the re-released *The Model* from **The Man-Machine**.

Unquestionably, **Autobahn** owes much of its long-standing appeal to an intelligent and considered translation of the capabilities of synthesisers. *Kometenmelodie 2* in compact style (at a mere 5 minutes) was the other big highlight on their futuristic LP from 1974.

100 GREAT ALBUM TRACKS 1980-89

1. ATROCITY EXHIBITION (**CLOSER**) - JOY DIVISION 1980
2. DEBASER (**DOOLITTLE**) – PIXIES 1989
3. ONCE IN A LIFETIME (**REMAIN IN LIGHT**) - TALKING HEADS 1980
4. YOU TRIP ME UP (**PSYCHOCANDY**) – THE JESUS AND MARY CHAIN 1985
5. BLUE MONDAY (**POWER, CORRUPTION & LIES**) - NEW ORDER 1983
6. WHAT DIFFERENCE DOES IT MAKE? (**THE SMITHS**) - THE SMITHS 1984
7. I AM THE RESURRECTION (**THE STONE ROSES**) - THE STONE ROSES 1989
8. SHE SELLS SANCTUARY (**LOVE**) – THE CULT 1985
9. WELCOME TO THE JUNGLE (**APPETITE FOR DESTRUCTION**) - GUNS N' ROSES 1987
10. SIGN O' THE TIMES (**SIGN O' THE TIMES**) – PRINCE 1987
11. EVERY BREATH YOU TAKE (**SYNCHRONICITY**) – THE POLICE 1983
12. THE BOYS OF SUMMER (**BUILDING THE PERFECT BEAST**) - DON HENLEY 1984
13. JUMP (**1984**) - VAN HALEN 1984
14. DOWNBOUND TRAIN (**BORN IN THE U.S.A.**) – BRUCE SPRINGSTEEN 1984
15. WHERE THE STREETS HAVE NO NAME (**THE JOSHUA TREE**) - U2 1987
16. THE MESSAGE (**THE MESSAGE**) – GRANDMASTER FLASH & THE FURIOUS FIVE 1982

17	ROCK THE CASBAH (**COMBAT ROCK**) – THE CLASH 1982
18	ACE OF SPADES (**ACE OF SPADES**) – MOTORHEAD 1980
19	START! (**SOUND AFFECTS**) – THE JAM 1980
20	SHOOT TO THRILL (**BACK IN BLACK**) - AC/DC 1980
21	SO. CENTRAL RAIN (**RECKONING**) - R.E.M. 1984
22	SLEDGEHAMMER (**SO**) - PETER GABRIEL 1986
23	ANIMAL (**HYSTERIA**) - DEF LEPPARD 1987
24	BEAT IT (**THRILLER**) - MICHAEL JACKSON 1982
25	WARDANCE (**KILLING JOKE**) - KILLING JOKE 1980
26	GIMME ALL YOUR LOVIN' (**ELIMINATOR**) - ZZ TOP 1983
27	ISOLATION (**CLOSER**) - JOY DIVISION 1980
28	WHEN DOVES CRY (**PURPLE RAIN**) - PRINCE & THE REVOLUTION 1984
29	PRIDE (IN THE NAME OF LOVE) (**THE UNFORGETTABLE FIRE**) - U2 1984
30	SHORE LEAVE (**SWORDFISHTROMBONES**) - TOM WAITS 1983
31	COMPUTER LOVE (**COMPUTER WORLD**) – KRAFTWERK 1981
32	LET'S DANCE (**LET'S DANCE**) - DAVID BOWIE 1983
33	DIAMONDS ON THE SOLES OF HER SHOES (**GRACELAND**) - PAUL SIMON 1986
34	RUNNING UP THAT HILL (A DEAL WITH GOD) (**HOUNDS OF LOVE**) - KATE BUSH 1985
35	FALLEN ANGEL (**ROBBIE ROBERTSON**) - ROBBIE ROBERTSON 1987
36	WORLD LEADER PRETEND (**GREEN**) - R.E.M. 1988

37	LIKE A PRAYER (**LIKE A PRAYER**) – MADONNA 1989	
38	RHYMIN' & STEALIN' (**LICENSED TO ILL**) - THE BEASTIE BOYS 1986	
39	HALLOWEEN PARADE (**NEW YORK**) - LOU REED 1989	
40	I STILL HAVEN'T FOUND WHAT I'M LOOKING FOR (**THE JOSHUA TREE**) – U2 1987	
41	I CAN'T STAND UP FOR FALLING DOWN (**GET HAPPY!!**) – ELVIS COSTELLO AND THE ATTRACTIONS 1980	
42	MY LITTLE UNDERGROUND (**PSYCHOCANDY**) – THE JESUS AND MARY CHAIN 1985	
43	DON'T RENEGE ON OUR LOVE (**SHOOT OUT THE LIGHTS**) – RICHARD & LINDA THOMPSON 1982	
44	POLITICAL WORLD (**OH MERCY**) – BOB DYLAN 1989	
45	DRIVE (**HEARTBEAT CITY**) – THE CARS 1984	
46	DON'T BELIEVE THE HYPE (**IT TAKES A NATION OF MILLIONS TO HOLD US BACK**) – PUBLIC ENEMY 1988	
47	ADDICTED TO LOVE (**RIPTIDE**) – ROBERT PALMER 1985	
48	OWNER OF A LONELY HEART (**90125**) – YES 1983	
49	WHO CAN IT BE NOW? (**BUSINESS AS USUAL**) - MEN AT WORK 1981	
50	WHY CAN'T THIS BE LOVE (**5150**) – VAN HALEN 1986	
51	WALK THIS WAY (**RAISING HELL**) – RUN-DMC (FEATURING AEROSMITH) 1986	
52	NO SURRENDER (**BORN IN THE U.S.A.**) - BRUCE SPRINGSTEEN 1984	

53 THE SICK BED OF CUCHULAINN (**RUM, SODOMY, AND THE LASH**) – THE POGUES 1985

54 DON'T YOU WANT ME (**DARE!**) – THE HUMAN LEAGUE 1981

55 NEED YOU TONIGHT (**KICK**) – INXS 1987

56 I.O.U. (**PLEASED TO MEET ME**) – THE REPLACEMENTS 1987

57 THE BOY WITH THE THORN IN HIS SIDE (**THE QUEEN IS DEAD**) – THE SMITHS 1986

58 HIGHWAY 61 (**THE BLASTERS**) – THE BLASTERS 1981

59 NEW YEAR'S DAY (**WAR**) – U2 1983

60 START ME UP (**TATTOO YOU**) - THE ROLLING STONES 1981

61 FAST CAR (**TRACY CHAPMAN**) - TRACY CHAPMAN 1988

62 LITTLE RED CORVETTE (**1999**) – PRINCE 1982

63 SHE BLINDED ME WITH SCIENCE (**THE GOLDEN AGE OF WIRELESS**) – THOMAS DOLBY 1982

64 THE HEALER (**THE HEALER**) – JOHN LEE HOOKER 1989

65 STEPPIN' OUT (**NIGHT AND DAY**) – JOE JACKSON 1982

66 COME ON EILEEN (**TOO-RYE-AY**) - DEXYS MIDNIGHT RUNNERS 1982

67 COULD YOU BE LOVED (**UPRISING**) – BOB MARLEY & THE WAILERS 1980

68 SILVER ROCKET (**DAYDREAM NATION**) – SONIC YOUTH 1988

69 O SUPERMAN (**BIG SCIENCE**) – LAURIE ANDERSON 1982

70   SWEET DREAMS (ARE MADE OF THIS) (**SWEET DREAMS (ARE MADE OF THIS)**) - EURYTHMICS 1983

71   COPPERHEAD ROAD (**COPPERHEAD ROAD**) – STEVE EARLE 1988

72   WINTER KILLS (**UPSTAIRS AT ERIC'S**) – YAZOO 1982

73   HAUNTS OF ANCIENT PEACE (**COMMON ONE**) – VAN MORRISON 1980

74   MIDNIGHT MOONLIGHT (**THE FIRM**) – THE FIRM 1985

75   MASTER OF PUPPETS (**MASTER OF PUPPETS**) – METALLICA 1986

76   LOVE BUZZ (**BLEACH**) – NIRVANA 1989

77   DON'T GO (**PEOPLE**) – HOTHOUSE FLOWERS 1988

78   DON'T DREAM IT'S OVER (**CROWDED HOUSE**) – CROWDED HOUSE 1986

79   MONEY FOR NOTHING (**BROTHERS IN ARMS**) – DIRE STRAITS 1985

80   THE WHOLE OF THE MOON (**THIS IS THE SEA**) – THE WATERBOYS 1985

81   THE NUMBER OF THE BEAST (**THE NUMBER OF THE BEAST**) – IRON MAIDEN 1982

82   THE LOOK OF LOVE (PART 1) (**THE LEXICON OF LOVE**) – ABC 1982

83   MOONLIGHT SHADOW (**CRISES**) – MIKE OLDFIELD 1983

84   ALIVE AND KICKING (**ONCE UPON A TIME**) – SIMPLE MINDS 1985

85   ALL FIRED UP (**WIDE AWAKE IN DREAMLAND**) - PAT BENATAR 1988

86   BLUE MOON REVISITED (SONG FOR ELVIS) (**THE TRINITY SESSION**) – COWBOY JUNKIES 1988

87 WOMAN (**DOUBLE FANTASY**) – JOHN LENNON & YOKO ONO 1980

88 PINK HOUSES (**UH-HUH**) – JOHN MELLENCAMP 1983

89 ICE (**ACADIE**) – DANIEL LANOIS 1989

90 WITH GOD ON OUR SIDE (**YELLOW MOON**) – THE NEVILLE BROTHERS 1989

91 MORE THAN THIS (**AVALON**) - ROXY MUSIC 1982

92 ME MYSELF & I (**3 FEET HIGH AND RISING**) – DE LA SOUL 1989

93 EVERYONE THINKS HE LOOKS DAFT (**GEORGE BEST**) – THE WEDDING PRESENT 1987

94 IT'S MY LIFE (**IT'S MY LIFE**) – TALK TALK 1984

95 ROCKIN' IN THE FREE WORLD (**FREEDOM**) – NEIL YOUNG 1989

96 RIP IT UP (**RIP IT UP**) – ORANGE JUICE 1982

97 SUMMER'S CAULDRON (**SKYLARKING**) – XTC 1986

98 DON'T STOP BELIEVIN' (**ESCAPE**) – JOURNEY 1981

99 INVISIBLE TOUCH (**INVISIBLE TOUCH**) – GENESIS 1986

100 FEED ME WITH YOUR KISS (**ISN'T ANYTHING**) – MY BLOODY VALENTINE 1988

(57)
(WHAT'S THE STORY) MORNING GLORY? – OASIS (1995)

(Hello/Roll With It/Wonderwall/Don't Look Back In Anger/Hey Now!/Some Might Say/Cast No Shadow/She's Electric/Morning Glory/Champagne Supernova)

Top Track: *Don't Look Back In Anger*

Their second album had a lot of public expectation to satisfy and initial thoughts on listening to the first track were not promising. *Hello* disastrously droned somewhere between flattering Slade circa *Far Far Away* and blatant plagiarism, *Hello Hello I'm Back Again* (Gary Glitter), neither being vital in the overall scheme of things. So, what were Oasis trying to say? Was the follow-up to **Definitely Maybe** a half-hearted celebration of a relatively forgettable era in British music? This being the opener to the most eagerly awaited record in ages, more was anticipated than a dire medley of re-worked glam rock hits.

The most famous Number 2 single since *Strawberry Fields Forever* only added to a sense of underachievement (*Roll With It*). The obvious detectable influence was prolific boogie band Status Quo (again, hardly worthy attendants in the hall of rock 'n' roll fame). Thus, two tracks in and ***(What's The Story) Morning Glory?*** was heading for a fatal fall. The turning point came next and from there onwards, the album was an absolute joy.

Anthems come in varying shapes and sizes, from complexity to simplicity, from heavy to soft. In *Wonderwall* (a reference to George Harrison's tentative solo effort from 1968) it didn't get much simpler or softer. In direct contrast to the tacky glam and 'Quoasis' start to the album *Wonderwall* spoke poignantly of undying love, commitment and passion. With its easy-going nature and plain-speaking verses, it's not difficult to understand why, for so many, it soon became viewed as the greatest love song ever. It was their appreciation of the plight of the downtrodden working class that helped Oasis to establish such a strong connection with the fans. You either loved them for putting arrogance (or self-confidence) back into rock or loathed their cocksure self-belief. Either way, you could not ignore the fact that they made great music.

Some pained over the systematic grave-digging through British musical ancestry, whilst aficionados were also troubled by 'minor' technicalities like the piano intro to *Don't Look Back In Anger*, claiming it borrowed too heavily from Lennon's *Imagine*. In truth, no influence was spared whether glam rock, Status Quo, Nirvana, Lennon or the Beatles. The title-track, for instance, owed more to the people's champion, Punk, but a brief paying of respects to late-seventies rock asides, Oasis mainly looked back thirty years, as sixties melodic cuts *She's Electric*, *Cast No Shadow* and *Champagne Supernova* testified. The monumental closing track dwarfed the rest of the set, in terms of musical range. Sounding like an escapee from **The Beatles** it began softly, gradually building into a magnificent tour-de-force, its lyrics continually searching for confession. Yes, it was ridiculously over-the-top and yet, it delivered a superb finale to an outstanding album – Britain's soundtrack for the final years of the 20th Century.

It provoked dissent in the music press, generally receiving a slating due to its emphasised nostalgic trips down memory lane. Not for the first time but rarely so noticeably, the critics were out of step with the ordinary music fan. How many people were deterred from buying the record after reading the reviews is incalculable but **(What's The Story) Morning Glory?** came in for an unfair lashing. Many respected reviewers were caught on the hop. Coming so soon after the awesome debut, more of the same was expected on this all-important 'difficult' second release. In many ways it was a particularly unique British characteristic – hype a band up to legend stature and then knock them down to size again.

(58)

URBAN HYMNS – THE VERVE (1997)

(Bitter Sweet Symphony/Sonnet/The Rolling People/The Drugs Don't Work/Catching The Butterfly/Neon Wilderness/Space And Time/Weeping Willow/Lucky Man/ One Day/This Time/Velvet Morning/Come On)

Top Track: *Bitter Sweet Symphony*

When the Verve called it a day in 1995 it was widely regarded that they had said their last goodbyes with the well-received ***A Northern Soul***. Within a year front man, Richard Ashcroft, re-formed the band but few speculators believed that the recording sessions for their third album would generate anything remotely as good. Remarkably, against a background of negativity and ill-ease, they sculptured a record that excelled even the wildest expectations.

The first inkling that something special was in the making came with the release of *Bitter Sweet Symphony*. With its catchy tune and addictive stringed intro (taken from Andrew Loog Oldham's orchestral rendition of the Rolling Stones hit *The Last Time*), it charmed its way into the heart and mind of the nation. Commanded by twisted but painfully truthful lyrics musing over life's hardships, together with an *Unfinished Sympathy* styled video, it effortlessly became the early summer anthem for 1997. Despite huge chart success they initially failed to receive royalties, with lawyers against them arguing that the string section took sampling further than acceptable. Nevertheless, it gave the Verve valuable publicity, bringing them to the attention of a wider audience and paving the way for massive album sales.

Urban Hymns met anticipations with something for everyone. For long-standing followers there was straight rock (*The Rolling People*, *Velvet Morning* and *Come On*), whilst for new fans there existed, what some described as middle-of-the-road material,

Sonnet, *One Day* and *Lucky Man*. The second single complied with the latter approach with its heavily acoustic treatment. *The Drugs Don't Work* was wrongly seen as being an anti-drugs warning message (purely based on its title) but, far from a *White Lines* for the nineties, it recalled Ashcroft's sadness during his father's dying days. Its heart-breaking verses, guided by a touching melody, placed many of life's problems into perspective.

Arguably, the re-occurring theme on **Urban Hymns** was 'existence' and more so, the mortality of us all. We cling to a belief that our presence in this world has some meaningful purpose and a wishful hope that redemption awaits in the next life. In the Verve's universe there was no atonement, no heaven or God, just a sober reality of the harsh present. References to yearning for salvation perpetually appeared, a call from heaven (*The Drugs Don't Work*), an absence of reassuring lullabies (*Space And Time*) and worryingly, an attempted conversation with God in a phone box on *Come On*. The sleeve to the single *History* (from **A Northern Soul**) stated – 'Life Is Not A Rehearsal' – rhetoric **Urban Hymns** explored fully.

(59)

MUSIC FOR THE JILTED GENERATION – THE PRODIGY (1994)

(***Intro/Break & Enter/Their Law/Full Throttle/Voodoo People/Speedway (Theme From Fastlane)/The Heat/Poison/No Good (Start The Dance)/One Love/3 Kilos/Skylined/Claustrophobic Sting***)

Top Track: Poison

Familiar with underground clubbers by way of their hits *Charly* and *Out Of Space*, the Prodigy strived for the big time in 1994, with their perfect for the moment second album. New laws devised by the Conservative Government (the Criminal Justice And Public Order Act 1994) were seen by many as curtailing rights, amongst which was staging Rave gatherings. The Prodigy seized the opportunity, seeking to speak on behalf of suppressed late-night ravers, whilst simultaneously moving the genre beyond its hardcore restraints. Demonstrating this point, the album's inner-cover featured a longhaired youth in confrontation with 'The Law'. In the absence of being allowed to pursue loud verbal protest, the rebellious hero used a one-fingered gesture of contempt for authority. There was more fighting talk in the linear notes, a passionate call-to-arms - all this without even putting the disc on! The real defiant quality, however, was in the music, a vibrant melting pot condensing modern British dance during the mid-nineties.

Intro (a 0:45 minute segment focused on tapping an old-fashioned typewriter) set out clearly the band's intent to move back underground. Fortunately, it was only a slight distraction before the true business kicked-in with the frantic, if somewhat lengthy, *Break & Enter*. *Their Law* left no doubts as to its topical debate, with a heated acknowledgement of modern society's disrespect for the law. Given the current socio-political climate in the country, and specifically in response to over-heated anti-Poll Tax clashes earlier in the decade, these were sentiments that summarised both UK youth circa 1994 and ordinary folk increasingly marginalised by the Government. More so it, together with the outrageously chaotic *Voodoo People*, innovatively swallowed strong guitar chords with fledgling Big-Beat. It was a potentially lethal combination that could have perilously fringed on disaster. The Prodigy's artful balancing act was a masterstroke of pure genius. Elsewhere, sporadic throwbacks to the fast evaporating Rave scene could be heard on *Speedway (Theme From Fastlane)* and the appropriately titled *Full Throttle*.

The interruption by a telephone call intrudes it seems, even musicians at work. No hardship done or loss to artistic creativity on this occasion, *Poison* not only was the highpoint but would become one of the decade's dance classics. Hugely inspirational, the crossover of African drumbeats, European synthesisers and UK attitudes brought admiration from budding rappers, rockers and post-ravers. Meanwhile, the unlikely hit single *No Good (Start*

The Dance) emerged as a youth anthem, gaining sizeable airplay on the increasingly radical MTV.

The final four cuts stuck to relatively conventional lines, Rave (*One Love*), Funk (*3 Kilos*), synthetic melodies circa Jean Michel Jarre (*Skylined*) and the anything goes finale (*Claustrophobic Sting*). It was a very long album to sit and listen to, but ideal for those late night parties.

(60)

GOODBYE YELLOW BRICK ROAD – ELTON JOHN (1973)

(*Funeral For A Friend/Love Lies Bleeding/Candle In The Wind/Bennie And The Jets/Goodbye Yellow Brick Road/ This Song Has No Title/Grey Seal/Jamaica Jerk-Off/I've Seen That Movie Too/ Sweet Painted Lady/The Ballad Of Danny Bailey (1909-34)/Dirty Little Girl/All The Girls Love Alice/Your Sister Can't Twist (But She Can Rock 'n' Roll)/ Saturday Night's Alright For Fighting/Roy Rogers/Social Disease/Harmony*)

Top Track: Love Lies Bleeding

The unstoppable rise of Elton John during the early-seventies could greatly be attributed to his excellent working relationship with songwriter Bernie Taupin. By 1973 his thoughtful lyrics and Elton's interpretation of them hit new highs with the double LP **Goodbye Yellow Brick Road**. Beginning with a synthesiser/piano instrumental, the set's emotional journey nonchalantly glided towards a broken heart on *Love Lies Bleeding*. Who in the world could not relate to this song's anguish over love in its darkest hours of reflection?

Were it not for tragedy in Paris on the last day of August 1997, *Candle In The Wind* would have remained merely a moving tribute to a Hollywood icon. First time out, the rose in question was the fallen heroine Marilyn Monroe. The loneliness of film culture's celebrated beauty star was stripped of fanfare and exposed dramatically with the tabloid announcement of her death – evidently the papers found greater mileage in the fact that she was found naked.

With so much association with death and bitterness, a welcome breather came with the humorous observations on life in the Caribbean, *Jamaica Jerk-Off*. With lyrics portraying low moral behaviour by the local population, this was clearly a time when the initials 'PC' were not connected with a restriction on expressive opinion.

The professional relationship between prostitutes and sailors disembarking for shore leave provided an unsavoury beginning to Side Three. On *Sweet Painted Lady* the contrasting odours of beer, sweat and sea air could almost be smelt. On **Don't Shoot Me I'm Only The Piano Player** Elton paid homage to the fifties with *Crocodile Rock* and it was to the same treasured era that *Your Sister Can't Twist (But She Can Rock 'n' Roll)* returned. Here music became elevated as high as heaven, where the dance floor was THE place to be. It marked only a brief flirtation with the simple pleasures found in good time fun. The album came thumping back down to earth with the troubles caused by alcohol on *Saturday Night's Alright For Fighting* and the even gloomier lost-hope heard on *Social Disease*.

Back in the seventies it made for a nice change to find the printed lyrics included with the cassette version. For too long considered an inferior alternative to vinyl, purchasers of compact tapes normally received a raw deal. Unlike their black-plastic competitors (accompanied by lyric sheets, posters and stickers), cassettes usually included nothing. Explanation for this lay in the impracticalities imposed by their size. **Goodbye Yellow Brick Road** at least made the effort, even if the lyric sheet's cumbersome nature resulted in an almighty push and shove to put it back in the cassette box when finished with.

(61)

SUPERUNKNOWN – SOUNDGARDEN (1994)

(*Let Me Drown/My Wave/Fell On Black Days/Mailman/ Superunknown/Head Down/Black Hole Sun/Spoonman/ Limo Wreck/The Day I Tried To Live/Kickstand/Fresh Tendrils/4th Of July/Half/Like Suicide/She Likes Surprises*)

Top Track: Superunknown

One of the surviving pioneers from the late-eighties Grunge movement, Soundgarden spectacularly defined the genre's strong influence by traditional rock on the dark and, at times, deeply sinister **Superunknown**. With sizeable chunks inspired by the seventies, these were songs bursting with spontaneous, electrifying chaos fronted by wilful, adulterous pleasures (musically!). With guitar riffs lifted from vintage Black Sabbath (for *Spoonman* insert *After Forever* from **Master Of Reality**), strong nerves were essential requirements for listening to their saturated menu containing depressive mania.

The sonic eruptions began with two screeching fireballs, *Let Me Drown* and *My Wave*, before sliding nicely into the first instalment of intense seriousness, coated with thick sludge, *Fell On Black Days*. Suicidal tendencies never strayed far from view, but paying too much attention to the lyrics served little justice to the rock heaven blasting from the tracks. It was a sheer pleasure to hear a band revelling in riffs and hooks, a triumphant celebration of the once lost art-form. The standout moment was the title-track, backed by *Head Down* - a fusion of stunning arrangements, beautifully gathering potions from rock and Folk (with a melody thrown in). Contrarily, 4th *Of July* found its spiritual home in the same murky undergrowth inhabited by their peers, Alice In Chains (Seattle's other finest purveyors of sad man's rock).

MTV still reigned as the chief TV outlet for broadcasting new videos and thanks to extensive coverage given to *Black Hole Sun*, Soundgarden reached the big league. A hefty 16 slabs of highly-explosive dynamite ensured that **Superunknown** entered the collections of only the strong-minded. Evidently the US in 1994 had many suitable fans, helping the record make an extremely credible debut at Number 1.

Unfairly ridiculed for sounding too much like one long, continuous rock chord from *Let Me Drown* through to *She Likes Surprises*, such criticism misses the point - **Superunknown** rocked with a savagery seldom heard since the seventies. Unsurprisingly, its appeal stretched beyond the Grunge fanclub and outwards to old-school rockers, being met with widespread critical approval.

(62)

UNPLUGGED IN NEW YORK – NIRVANA (1994)

(About A Girl/Come As You Are/Jesus Doesn't Want Me For A Sunbeam/The Man Who Sold The World/Pennyroyal Tea/Dumb/Polly/On A Plain/Something In The Way/ Plateau/Oh Me/Lake Of Fire/All Apologies/Where Did You Sleep Last Night?)

Top Track: *Where Did You Sleep Last Night?*

The best thing about MTV during the nineties was its Unplugged series, whereby musicians re-worked popular material within the framework of an acoustic setting. There were many superb performances, notably by Neil Young, Eric Clapton and surprisingly, given the robust nature of their music, Alice In Chains. The best was the Nirvana 'concert' recorded at Sony Studios, New York on the evening of 18 November 1993.

The idea of the Grunge monsters converting their pop-powered rock into a format suitable for a cosy, intimate small venue was, at first thought, unachievable. For a start, disregarding the compilation **Incesticide**, the band only had three albums under their belt, with the bulk of their songs hardly prime candidates for a low-key environment. Realising the necessity to borrow from others to make an evening of the occasion, they enlisted a series of covers that intriguingly gave an insight into their influences.

The performance began with moving renditions of *About A Girl* (from **Bleach**) and *Come As You Are* (from **Nevermind**), both showing that Nirvana's music had all along contained softer touches. There were clues as to what, or specifically who, had inspired Kurt Cobain to become a rock star. David Bowie's *The Man Who Sold The World* was transformed, likewise Huddie Ledbetter's, *Where Did You Sleep Last Night?*, with the painfully despondent singer producing his most emotional screams of the night.

Old friends, the Meat Puppets, made guest appearances on tracks they had written years earlier, (*Plateau*, *Oh Me* and *Lake Of Fire* were in keeping with the eeriness), whilst *Jesus Doesn't Want Me For A Sunbeam*, *Polly* and *Dumb* mirrored the rapidly deteriorating state of Cobain's mind. Ironically, for this evening he was uncharacteristically jovial, cracking jokes, smiling and laughing. Behind this optimistic exterior lay a defeated man, uncomfortable with his icon status and on the verge of a personal catastrophe. The alarm bells were already ringing but few realised just how bad things were. His suicide in April 1994 resulted in the song selections being scrutinised, as tell-tell signs were searched for. Better than any live album because of its dramatic intensity, **Unplugged In New York** still brings tears to the eyes and troubled thoughts to the mind.

(63)
EVERYTHING MUST GO – MANIC STREET PREACHERS (1996)

(Elvis Impersonator: Blackpool Pier/A Design For Life/ Kevin Carter/Enola Alone/Everything Must Go/Small Black Flowers That Grow In The Sky/The Girl Who Wanted To Be God/ Removables/Australia/Interiors (Song For Willem De Kooning)/Further Away/No Surface All Feeling)

Top Track: *A Design For Life*

Welsh rockers Manic Street Preachers aspired to the commercial bright lights with ***Everything Must Go***, crossing over from entertainment for depressed students to the big time. For many, the most famous aspect about them had, hitherto, been the disappearance of their main songwriter and public focal point, Richey Edwards. With a reputation for self-mutilation, coupled with episodes of mental illness, it came as no surprise to those closest to him that he could contemplate a dramatic conclusion to his pitiful life. To this day, events surrounding his demise remain shrouded in mystery, although the general consensus is that he is no longer with us. He left behind a lasting legacy, including five tracks recorded by the surviving members for their fourth album.

As far as significant changes in musical fundamentals go, they don't get much bigger than this. ***The Holy Bible*** (1994) was a stark affair driven by disturbing, controversial 'food-for-thought' lyrics (topics included the Holocaust, nihilism and politics), ensuring strong support amongst disillusioned souls in bedsit land. In contrast, the new record was a highly-polished batch of twelve pristine tunes, none excessively lengthy and all were free from filler.

The marvellous semi-Pop lead single, *A Design For Life*, came as a horrifying shock to dedicated fans accustomed to the abrasive nature of the band's earlier releases. For them, the song's sugar-sweetness smacked of selling-out, an act of betrayal. For the impartial, for whom the name Manic Street Preachers had until now meant little, it represented a satisfying 'introduction'. *Australia, Kevin Carter* and the title-track were also released as '45s' but tucked away on the set were flashes of pure simplicity, typically the opener *Elvis Impersonator: Blackpool Pier* and the quaint *Small Black Flowers That Grow In The Sky*.

The big question was this. Had MSP sacrificed their ground level fanbase in order to gain from the rewards of mainstream popularity? Powerful rock such as *Further Away, Enola/Alone* and *Everything Must Go*, together with the fist-in-the-sky anthem *No Surface All Feeling* suggested not too much had really been lost from their philosophy. There had merely been a realigning of approach. Not without good reason did **Everything Must Go** get voted the best album of 1996 by just about every respected music magazine in Britain (Q/Select/Vox/Sky for starters).

(64)

LED ZEPPELIN (1969)

(***Good Times Bad Times/Babe I'm Gonna Leave You/You Shook Me/Dazed And Confused/Your Time Is Gonna Come/Black Mountain Side/Communication Breakdown/I Can't Quit You Baby/How Many More Times***)

Top Track: Dazed And Confused

At a time when groups were spending an eternity in recording sessions striving for perfection, it epitomised Led Zeppelin's collective urgency that their debut LP was recorded in less than forty studio hours. The song choices, many of which were already well-rehearsed and performed during their recent Scandinavian tour, unquestionably assisted with this economical efficiency. Despite a barrage of negative reviews **Led Zeppelin** was an immediate success, especially in America where the 45

Communication Breakdown/Good Times Bad Times benefited from extensive radio airplay. Speed was the byword for their music, with their single exemplifying lightning-paced creativity.

Good Times Bad Times, at face value, was just another scorned-love story, with Robert Plant hollering his heartbreak, but it was Jimmy Page's solo that gave this set such a memorable start. *Communication Breakdown* lasted barely 150 seconds but covered more ground than most bands manage in a career. If ever there was the archetypal HM track, this was it! Between them they were the perfect advertisement for the mother album's serious credentials.

Babe I'm Gonna Leave You began so innocently, lazy and pastoral. Then, just when it seemed that the raw energy unleashed on the opening cut had subsided, the momentum soared once more – thumping drumbeats by John Bonham, Plant's vocals piercing the skyline, together with Page and John Paul Jones complementing the electrical hurricane, made this an early Led Zeppelin juggernaut to remember. The centrepiece was *Dazed And Confused* with its mournful/despising tale of frustrated love. Showcasing individual talents, from the haunting bass introduction, Page and Bonham's emphatic force through to venomous cries bemoaning a woman's devilish soul, this was all about taking rock music towards heavy storms and unchartered waters. Check out the tempestuous mid-sequence as Page and Plant battle in combat, matching each other's best efforts to make the wildest screeches.

Improvisational techniques and considerable 'borrowing' (*You Shook Me* and *I Can't Quit You Baby* were Chicago Blues legend Willie Dixon chestnuts) put down a blueprint that produced scores of imitators. Approval to the album in the UK was initially muted, but over in the States the band's HM bombardment was greeted with tremendous enthusiasm. It was not until **Led Zeppelin II** that Britain finally caught up.

(65)

THE VELVET UNDERGROUND (1969)

(*Candy Says/What Goes On/Some Kinda Love/Pale Blue Eyes/Jesus/Beginning To See The Light/I'm Set Free/ That's The Story Of My Life/The Murder Mystery/After Hours*)

Top Track: Candy Says

In March 1969 New York's finest exponents of late-sixties art-rock, now minus bass guitarist John Cale, released their third LP. Unlike the debut, where mesmerising guitar riffs induced adrenalin surges, or their second, **White Light/White Heat**, on which a deafening racket obscured any commercial viability, **The Velvet Underground** signalled a shift towards a more mellow sound.

Although there was an apparent change in ethos, there remained a VU trademark for composing songs that, at times, verged on manic-depressive. On *Candy Says* worrying conclusions were reached, a sense of self-hate, whilst later Lou Reed confessed to an upside down lifestyle enjoying wine in the mornings, saving breakfast for his evenings (*Beginning To See The Light*). During moments of personal desperation the most anti-religious can still find themselves seeking help from divine spirits, with even the street-wise VU making a dedicated plea to one icon, *Jesus*. It was a long way from the odes to heroin and sadomasochistic sex heard on their debut.

These were songs more than capable of holding their own in the singles chart, precisely in tune with radio programming dictates. Easily their most marketable album from the trio released in the sixties, it should have broken them into the top division. Alas, the few that took notice when **The Velvet Underground & Nico** arrived in record stores during early 1967 were less in number after hearing the noise assault **White Light/White Heat**. By the time of ***The Velvet Underground*** the band's followers had dwindled still further. Sadly, a beautiful folksy album (excusing the nonsensical *The Murder Mystery*) was left begging for an audience. A year later the end beckoned, with Reed sticking around to play a part in one final LP before pursuing an inconsistent solo career. It could have been so different, if only greater attention was paid to a group that subsequently influenced more bands than probably any.

(66)

BACK IN BLACK – AC/DC (1980)

(***Hells Bells/Shoot To Thrill/What Do You Do For Money Honey/Givin The Dog A Bone/Let Me Put My Love Into You/Back In Black/You Shook Me All Night Long/Have A Drink On Me/Shake A Leg/Rock And Roll Ain't Noise Pollution***)

Top Track: *Shoot To Thrill*

The name ***Back In Black***, packaged by an austere sleeve, suggested that the surviving members of AC/DC were still in mourning over the recent death of their lead singer, Bon Scott. To the contrary, the music and lyrics displayed a commitment to good-time, earthly pleasures (sex and booze), defined by an embedded philosophy that life goes on. Predictably, the band's seventh studio LP was met with uncertainty, from Scott fanatics and over-sensitive critics, with numerous complaints levied at the lyrical content and an obvious influence by early-seventies rockers. Were AC/DC guilty of stealing from British rock's foundations, or was this purely a pilgrimage visit?

The morbid theme depicted by the album's title set the initial tone to the opening track, with its bell-tolling, almost funeral-styled ambience. Even when the drums started, followed by Brian Johnson's introduction to the AC/DC multitudes, there was no avoiding a feeling that they were not for rushing. Concerns by the faithful that a new, slower AC/DC had been born were quickly sent smashing skywards when track two pressed the ignition button. *Shoot To Thrill* was a top rate demonstration on how a good rock song should sound - riffs to die for, masculine lyrics of wisdom and fast-flowing power at its very best.

What Do You Do For Money Honey and *Givin The Dog A Bone* adhered to a party-boogie notion, providing head-bangers with a much needed fix. The first let-up didn't come until *Let Me Put My Love Into You* (leaving nothing to the imagination) and the title-track's rhythmic funkadelics. Order was restored with *You Shook Me All Night Long*, as hooks & riffs resumed, together with a chorus sure to get the unconverted fans doing their Johnson impersonations. The run-in to album's end consistently stayed with route one action-packed tunes, reaching a vigorous finale on the self-congratulatory *Rock And Roll Ain't Noise Pollution* (which is true, of course). The late-seventies/early-eighties were a period of transition. From this era there are few truly spectacular rock long-players, but here's one.

(67)

EVERYBODY KNOWS THIS IS NOWHERE – NEIL YOUNG (1969)

(***Cinnamon Girl/Everybody Knows This Is Nowhere/Round & Round (It Won't Be Long)/Down By The River/The Losing End (When You're On)/Running Dry/Cowgirl In The Sand***)

Top Track: *Down By The River*

The quality of Young's songwriting within Buffalo Springfield offered many reasons for an optimistic future for the young Canadian. Hopes were high that after the band's split in 1968 it wouldn't be long before his solo career materialised substantial rewards. A lacklustre debut, however, gave cause for concern, with little found to match his promising reputation. **Neil Young** paled into insignificance in comparison with its landmark follow-up.

A group of musicians, collectively known as Crazy Horse, jammed with Young on the three tracks that gave **Everybody Knows This Is Nowhere** its strong backbone. The first, *Cinnamon Girl*, captures him contemplating positively, looking forward to the future. At just 2:58 minutes it was short and concise, a happy rocking start that deceptively paved the path for escapist wishes (the title-track) and thoughtful reflection (*Round & Round*). It was, however, the lengthier compositions (these being the second and third supported by Crazy Horse) that make Young's second LP so brilliant.

Down By The River and *Cowgirl In The Sand* between them weighed in at almost twenty minutes and in true late-sixties, 'dropping-out' mode, entranced the listener to a position of horizontalness. Explanation for this laid-back approach arguably lay in Young's actual state of mind whilst writing them. Almost passing-out in Topanga Canyon with a high temperature, he rested in bed. Seemingly there was little else he could do, other than compose music for sleep-inducement via hypnotic chord arrangements. Both songs had few lyrics, with a belief that they existed purely to punctuate the guitar workouts.

Down By The River typified hippydom ideology, featuring rapturously eternal gaps separating each verse, layered by unhurried solos. Young sang in his inimitable way, his high-pitch vocals close on bursting eardrums, yet infectiously intriguing. In the wrong hands such a lengthy song would have stumbled towards a preposterous mess, an arduous ordeal, but these were the hands of a master craftsman. *Down By The River* remains woefully overlooked by too many music fans.

Cowgirl In The Sand was slightly faster but, again, Young takes his time to make his point. Lyrically awash with cryptic statements, you couldn't get away from feeling that his vocals were superfluous, his adaptation with the guitar emerging as his real 'voice'. Including two expansive works on one album was ambitiously courageous, particularly in view of the failings of his debut on which a nine minutes-plus track (*The Last Trip To Tulsa*) highlighted its many deficiencies.

Young's self-belief was justified and far from being nowhere, he had finally landed. A career that came close to floundering on the rocks was rescued from the brink. Using Crazy Horse as his backing band became a reoccurring theme throughout the subsequent decades. It's worthy of note that whenever he did, it coincided with his finest releases.

(68)

NEW YORK – LOU REED (1989)

(*Romeo Had Juliette/Halloween Parade/Dirty Blvd/Endless Cycle/There Is No Time/Last Great American Whale/ Beginning Of A Great Adventure/Busload Of Faith/Sick Of You/Hold On/Good Evening Mr Waldheim/Xmas In February/Strawman/Dime Store Mystery*)

Top Track: Halloween Parade

Peaking early in his post-Velvet Underground career with **Transformer** (1972) and **Berlin** (1973), the next 16 years became an abyss for Punk's godfather. After this lengthy period of relative obscurity, Lou Reed 'returned' in 1989 with his best solo work.

New York rummaged through the Big Apple's gutters and sewers, uncovering sardonic characters, miserable hardships and an eagerness to leave no stone unturned, debating a plethora of controversial issues. Rarely had child abuse and marital breakdown come in for such a defeatist assessment as it did on the fraught with tempered emotion *Endless Cycle*. Equally, at a time when society at large wrestled with the long-term implications of AIDS,

Reed showed that personal dimensions to the widening tragedy existed (*Halloween Parade*). Here could be found a heartfelt acknowledgment, a simple tribute to a dearly missed friend no longer around. Cinderellas and drags painted a colourful gala of queens, but the sombre message of the disease's impact on the gay community was unequivocal. Similarly, industrialisation's harm on the fragile environment was underscored on *Last Great American Whale* (launching a scathing attack on polluters).

The tracks flowed seamlessly, like a continuous suite performed by a conventional rock band (a singer, drummer, bass and electric guitarist forming the core components to the basic line-up). The songs were recorded in the same running order appearing on the album. According to the accompanying notes, it was important to listen to them in one 'sitting', as though a book or a movie. Not a happy book or film by any stretch of the imagination but as a series of songs, it took some beating.

It was highly appropriate that the lyrical stories navigated through the Bronx, the 'Statue of Bigotry' and the Great Lakes. Yet, all the time, New York City remained the place where Reed's heart belonged, in amongst garbage cans, syringes and broken glass. Strangely, given that the songs were sung in English, the lyric sheet was written in five languages. It wasn't quite the same listening to them and following the words using the foreign versions! What was the point?

(69)

POWER, CORRUPTION & LIES – NEW ORDER (1983)

(*Age Of Consent/We All Stand/The Village/5 8 6/Blue Monday/Your Silent Face/Ultraviolence/Ecstasy/Leave Me Alone/The Beach*)

Top Track: Blue Monday

After a brief mourning period following the suicide of Ian Curtis in May 1980, Joy Division set about reinventing themselves. Honouring an agreement to discontinue using the band name in the event of someone leaving, New Order arose from the charred ashes. A flawed debut album struggled to break free from the shackles imposed by their former lead singer/lyricist's ghost. Their second attempt, **Power, Corruption & Lies**, was a far stronger performance, maintaining the mystique that shrouded Joy Division, whilst pushing towards musical boundaries that held greater commercial promise.

Age Of Consent encapsulated this new approach. Guided by predominant bass licks competing against blazing synthesisers, and with Bernard Sumner's vocals commanding respect, a stumbling career was rekindled. *We All Stand* found their previous incarnation resurrected in haunting familiarity, whilst *5 8 6* served obediently as the stepping-stone to the electro/dance anthem that defined an era.

Blue Monday, the breakthrough 45, sought influences from a wide range (including Kraftwerk and Donna Summer), gaining popularity amongst post-Punk 'industrialists' and new romantic dance-goers. Mainstream recognition followed, the term 'crossover-hit' was tagged and, although originally only available on the costly 12" format, the single took up residency in the UK chart for nearly six months. This success was undoubtedly assisted by the decision not to include it on the UK version of the album (although subsequent re-issues soon addressed this marketing tactic). As for whom *Blue Monday* was about? The suitably ambiguous lyrics did make you wonder.

Entrusting Sumner with lead vocal duties had appeared ill-judged on **Movement** (1981) but now there were signs of growing maturity. Singing in a flat tone, intent on pronouncing each syllable distinctly, his technique felt so Continental European. In essence, imitation was the highest form of flattery towards New Order's German mentors. *Your Silent Face* took the paying of respects to 'Kraut rock' fully overboard with a carbon copy of Kraftwerk's unique style. Again, the English spoken like a German was prominent, although the song's closing remark ultimately gave the singer's true origins away, with a blunt request for the unwelcome visitor to go away!

Only New Order could respectfully take the damaged seeds planted by Ian Curtis and cultivate them into a refreshing sound appealing to the masses. Embracing the twin cultures of contemporary electronic dance and underground ideologies, they 'progressed' to higher levels of success. Subsequent releases, however, suffered from a betrayal of everything that Joy Division stood for, with popular approval gained at sincerity's expense. Second only to the death of their inspirational leader in 1980, is the tragedy that New Order transformed into a Pop machine.

(70)

DIRT – ALICE IN CHAINS (1992)
(*Them Bones/Dam That River/Rain When I Die/Down In A Hole/ Sickman/Rooster/Junkhead/Dirt/God Smack/Iron Gland/Hate To Feel/Angry Chair/Would?*)

Top Track: Would?

Grunge tightened its stranglehold on the US scene during 1992 with a relentless procession of bands hell-bent on creating tidal waves of violent sounding rock. The darkest, scariest and most godforsaken purveyors, Alice In Chains, produced a genuine riffs masterpiece, **Dirt**. Likewise with Nirvana, Black Sabbath were immediately identifiable as a major source for ideas but, whereas **Nevermind** gleamed with manipulative hooks and hummable pop tunes, Alice In Chains leaned towards conventional rock lines.

There was little happiness on these 13 brutal songs, just strong electrifying pulses conquered by lyrical themes fixated on self-pity, drugs, death and all-out misery. Right from the off *Them Bones* launched a ferocious terror assault with lead singer, Layne Staley, growling a litany of self-prophecy doom. The almost non-existent gap between this and *Dam That River* left no chance to pause for thought before further intense, dramatic pyrotechnics ensued, in conjunction with another aggressive verbal outburst.

Everything was doused with foreboding gloom and furious disillusionment ignited by narcotic abuse. Disturbing thoughts became public knowledge at every opportunity, with several tracks (specifically *Sickman, Junkhead* and *Angry Chair*) dealing with heroin addiction. Even on the slower cuts such as *Rooster* and *Down In A Hole* the grim-reaper never strayed far from view. The Black Sabbath circa **Paranoid** fascination seriously reached obsessive proportions on *Rain When I Die, Dirt, God Smack* and *Hate To Feel*.

In much the same way that Brit Pop in the mid-nineties found its allegiances with young and old, so too Grunge's heavy core gained respect and admiration amongst a sizeable age-range. **Dirt** was as good as many heavy rock giants from the seventies.

(71)

THE RISING - BRUCE SPRINGSTEEN (2002)

(Lonesome Day/Into The Fire/Waitin' On A Sunny Day/ Nothing Man/Countin' On A Miracle/Empty Sky/Worlds Apart/Let's Be Friends (Skin To Skin)/Further On (Up The Road)/The Fuse/ Mary's Place/You're Missing/The Rising/Paradise/My City Of Ruins)

Top Track: The Rising

Anyone old enough to remember those shocking TV images of two aeroplanes slamming in to the WTC, pitiful bodies leaping from windows to a terrifying death, the North and South towers collapsing in a crumpled heap, will never forget 9/11. Only God could know what went through the minds of the innocent passengers, those in the upper towers and the thoughts too of the firemen that perished in the fires. Yes, only God and where was he on that terrible day?

Soon enough a songwriter was going to tackle the many sensitive issues arising from 9/11. Fortunately, that someone with a quest to shape order from the chaos and carnage was America's famed modern poet of urban apprehensions, Bruce Springsteen. For the first time since 1984 The Boss and the E-Street Band had something to say.

The first mystery to decipher was why the title-track didn't occupy the key, opening slot. That's clearly where it belonged, laying down the itinerary from the start. Its title suggested a call-to-arms agenda but closer inspection of the lyrics revealed that there was no wish for retaliation - this was a time for reflection. More so, this was also a moment to pay tribute and respect to one, of many, heroic firemen going about their duties. It signified Springsteen's search to uncover personal stories from a collective disaster, to strip away the statistics (four planes, two towers, one Pentagon, over 3,000 fatalities) and unmask individual suffering.

The prestigious opening track honour was bestowed on the single, *Lonesome Day*. Springsteen had a specific message for anyone intent on revenge, namely that they should ask probing questions first before embarking on an angry response. The semi-Gospel/Folk-tinged *Into The Fire* (further commemorations dedicated to the NYFD) also needed no clarification. The lyrics were only too self-evident, with images of a sky falling, blood, dust and stairs. It was a painful reminder of a sunny September morning shattered by evil's visitation.

Nothing Man reflected worries by a war veteran, but equally echoed sentiments by an unsung hero from 9/11. Drawing attention to misgivings regarding the War on Terrorism instigated by the Bush Administration, *Worlds Apart* charmed with its duel influences by contemporary (US) and traditional rhythms (from a Middle Eastern origin). Springsteen's shrewd observations were taking heed of surging US military power, already used in anger to topple the Taliban in Afghanistan (2001), and during 2002 in the process of turning on Iraq.

Two upbeat tunes, the inconsequential *Let's Be Friends (Skin To Skin)* and *Further On (Up The Road)*, made for an unwanted diversion from the serious job in hand. *Mary's Place* put things back on course, it was as if The Boss was keen to re-live the good old days before terrorism destroyed America's insulation - but everything kept coming back to one day. *You're Missing*, the inspirational title-track, *Paradise* and *My City Of Ruins* finalised a traumatic listening experience. With several literary references to 9/11 Springsteen had a difficult balancing act to consider, but achieved his modern classic with ease.

(72)

DESERTER'S SONGS – MERCURY REV (1998)

(*Holes/Tonite It Shows/Endlessly/I Collect Coins/Opus 40/Hudson Line/The Happy End (The Drunk Room)/ Goddess On A Hiway/The Funny Bird/Pick Up If You're There/Delta Sun Bottleneck Stomp*)

Top Track: Opus 40

By decree of New Musical Express in their year-end assessments, this was the best album released during 1998. It made no use of sampling or re-writing of golden oldies but instead revealed eleven assorted cuts of the utmost beauty. This wasn't to say that originality ruled supreme because in the case of Mercury Rev, an overpowering apparition from the Band lurked around every corner. Legitimacy was, however, afforded with contributions by former Band members on two tracks - drums on *Opus 40* performed by Levon Helm and alto sax/tenor on *Hudson Line* by Garth Hudson.

Jonathan Donahue's words were an intellectual challenge taxing lovers of cryptic, at times strange, verses. Even with the assistance of a printed lyric sheet it was still difficult deciphering what they were about. *Holes* was a slow mover with an almost ghostly presence that flowed over to *Tonite It Shows* and *Endlessly*. Surrealism entombed in a mysterious dream united the trio, but rising above craziness to make coherence of it all was the music, sounding like it had been born in a twilight land. Particularly on *Endlessly* a lullaby mood of younger days was evoked, a time of innocence, whilst lyrically a schizophrenic terror prevailed.

Nothing, however, could prepare the world for the ethereal treasure *Opus 40*, entwined with shocking images of wrists being scratched in the rain. If suicide acted as a questionable form of desertion, there were no harboured doubts on the fast getaway

Hudson Line, defined by a hasty departure using a one-way ticket. Underscoring escapist goals, the music ironically touched on scintillating pleasures derived from rock's purer years. **Deserter's Songs** wasn't an obvious place to go looking for hit singles but *Goddess On A Hiway* and the knees-up, semi-dance *Delta Sun Bottleneck Stomp* were exactly that.

'Magnificent', 'beautiful', 'stratospheric' and 'sentimental' were just some descriptions rightfully expressed by critics. At a time when bands had become obsessed with delving into big beats and guitar renaissance, the only way to appreciate Mercury Rev's career zenith was to turn the lights out, sit back and let the music enchant.

(73)

L.A. WOMAN – THE DOORS (1971)

(The Changeling/Love Her Madly/Been Down So Long/ Cars Hiss By My Window/L.A. Woman/L'America/ Hyacinth House/Crawling King Snake/The WASP (Texas Radio And The Big Beat)/Riders On The Storm)

Top Track: *Riders On The Storm*

Jim Morrison had to break away from the pressures imposed by the media spotlight and crucially before it was too late. In March 1971 he moved to Paris, finding refuge by walking through the French capital's cobbled streets and outdoor markets. Such welcome contentment wasn't to last, with an ominously dark depression, exacerbated by excessive alcohol consumption, clouding his days. Four months later, on July 3rd, he died in circumstances that remain mystifying.

Fans in denial looked to 'meaningful' lyrics for last-chance hope that he was still alive. Rock scholars also commented that the wayward icon had often touted the idea of staging a pretend death to generate publicity for the Doors. The reality, sadly, was that he had pushed himself beyond reasonable endurance, and his body simply gave up the ghost.

Consolation could be taken from his first-class finale, **L.A. Woman**, released just weeks before his demise. The best album by the Doors since their debut, it contained the same sugar-coated pop characteristics of earlier releases (*Love Her Madly*), hard-punching rock (*The Changeling*), whilst burrowing deep down in to traditional Blues (*Cars Hiss By My Window*). On the title-track Morrison spoke of Mr Mojo in a manner suggesting a re-birth, a sense of renewal, causing speculators to insist that this was a clue pointing towards his fake death. Conclusive evidence of a messiah resurrection it wasn't, but beyond reproach was the song's effervescent pop fusion with rock's primal aggression.

The moody *Riders On The Storm* began with the sound of rain, thunder and tormenting bass licks, enhanced by Ray Manzarek's poltergeist accompaniment on the electric piano. The words read like a ghastly nursery rhyme with haunting references to an actor and killer, yet as though sung by a spirit from the next life. It was chilling, the band's interaction between instrument and vocalist inducing a cold sweat. The last track recorded by the Doors with their leader at the helm, it received strong criticism from purists complaining it was a 'cocktail music' sell-out. To others, it marked a fitting farewell by a true talisman.

That he died so young, still great and so bizarrely, allowed a mystique to form, fuelling a lasting legacy. He also left one burning 'what if?' question unanswered, forever. Imagine new work by Jim Morrison and the Doors being released in 1972, 1973… what would it have sounded like?

(74)

THE FACTS OF LIFE – BLACK BOX RECORDER (2000)

(*The Art Of Driving/Weekend/The English Motorway System/May Queen/Sex Life/French Rock 'N' Roll/The Facts Of Life/Straight Life/Gift Horse/The Deverell Twins/ Goodnight Kiss*)

Top Track: *The Facts Of Life*

With its breathtaking infusion of quintessential French-styled Electronica, coupled with ricocheting heavenly tunes, Black Box Recorder's second album was a sheer joy. THAT sound, so reminiscent of Saint Etienne, provided a wonderful backdrop for songs eager to explore sexual awakening. *The Art Of Driving*, for instance, travelled along a series of innocently bungled mishaps, where innuendo suitably described novice exploration (driving or otherwise) by two fledgling discoverers.

In an equally dual-tracked storyline, *The English Motorway System* transformed the dreariness of motorway journeys into something beautiful. A lonesome guitar introduced *May Queen*, supported by the band's secret weapon, Sarah Nixey's arousing vocals. It was pure English countryside-rendezvous sauciness, but did this song hide something more sinister? *Sex Life* ventured into the frustrated dreams of a mind begging for it, whilst *French Rock 'N' Roll* swooned to Nixey's narrative sultriness; the latter was pollinated by romantic instrumentation and chiming bells, so insatiable, hearing this was as good as the real thing.

The title-track dealt with a mother's realisation that her two young sons were developing sexual imaginations. Once again, BBR applied childlike simplicity to their song construction, making an endearing impression. Similar radiant touches coated *Straight Life*, with a gorgeous chorus hook, whilst *Gift Horse* took a basic, universal message of wanting to be loved, and made it a heartfelt plea. *Goodnight Kiss* signed-off with a further 'tribute' to the aural pleasures that normally only Saint Etienne could master - superb!

There were no unnecessary inclusions, no lengthy, tiresome tracks or over-the-top guitar solos. Fortunately, it came with two album covers. The outer cardboard sleeve pictured the smartly-dressed, sophisticated trio (Luke Haines, John Moore and Sarah Nixey). Slide this away and a miserable teenager sneering in front of a butcher's rack of carcasses awaited. Further ghastly imageries were found on the inner-sleeve but ignore all that and listen to the CD, because every tune is impossibly adorable.

100 GREAT ALBUM TRACKS 1990-99

1. SMELLS LIKE TEEN SPIRIT (**NEVERMIND**) – NIRVANA 1991
2. ROCK 'N' ROLL STAR (**DEFINITELY MAYBE**) – OASIS 1994
3. STREET SPIRIT (FADE OUT) (**THE BENDS**) – RADIOHEAD 1995
4. LOADED (**SCREAMADELICA**) - PRIMAL SCREAM 1991
5. BITTER SWEET SYMPHONY (**URBAN HYMNS**) - THE VERVE 1997
6. LA FEMME D'ARGENT (**MOON SAFARI**) - AIR 1998
7. SOON (**LOVELESS**) – MY BLOODY VALENTINE 1991
8. A DESIGN FOR LIFE (**EVERYTHING MUST GO**) - MANIC STREET PREACHERS 1996
9. ROADS (**DUMMY**) – PORTISHEAD 1994
10. THE BARTENDER AND THE THIEF (**PERFORMANCE AND COCKTAILS**) – STEREOPHONICS 1999
11. UNFINISHED SYMPATHY (**BLUE LINES**) - MASSIVE ATTACK 1991
12. HOW HIGH (**TELLIN' STORIES**) - THE CHARLATANS 1997
13. LAST GOODBYE (**GRACE**) – JEFF BUCKLEY 1994
14. CONNECTED (**CONNECTED**) - STEREO MCS 1992
15. MAN ON THE MOON (**AUTOMATIC FOR THE PEOPLE**) - R.E.M. 1992
16. STEP ON (**PILLS 'N' THRILLS & BELLYACHES**) - HAPPY MONDAYS 1990
17. ROCK MUSIC (**BOSSANOVA**) – PIXIES 1990

18	PUT THE MESSAGE IN THE BOX (**GOODBYE JUMBO**) - WORLD PARTY 1990	
19	SUN HITS THE SKY (**IN IT FOR THE MONEY**) – SUPERGRASS 1997	
20	POISON (**MUSIC FOR THE JILTED GENERATION**) – THE PRODIGY 1994	
21	PARANOID ANDROID (**OK COMPUTER**) – RADIOHEAD 1997	
22	DON'T LOOK BACK IN ANGER (**(WHAT'S THE STORY) MORNING GLORY?**) – OASIS 1995	
23	CHANGE (**JOLLIFICATION**) – THE LIGHTNING SEEDS 1994	
24	EVEN BETTER THAN THE REAL THING (**ACHTUNG BABY**) - U2 1991	
25	GOIN' BACK TO HARLAN (**WRECKING BALL**) – EMMYLOU HARRIS 1995	
26	DISARM (**SIAMESE DREAM**) – THE SMASHING PUMPKINS 1993	
27	HIGHER THAN THE SUN (**SCREAMADELICA**) - PRIMAL SCREAM 1991	
28	PRIVATE UNIVERSE (**TOGETHER ALONE**) - CROWDED HOUSE 1993	
29	NOT IF YOU WERE THE LAST JUNKIE ON EARTH (**... THE DANDY WARHOLS COME DOWN**) - THE DANDY WARHOLS 1997	
30	RAY OF LIGHT (**RAY OF LIGHT**) – MADONNA 1998	
31	FIRESTARTER (**THE FAT OF THE LAND**) – THE PRODIGY 1997	
32	WOULD? (**DIRT**) - ALICE IN CHAINS 1992	
33	DON'T GO AWAY (**BE HERE NOW**) – OASIS 1997	
34	COME AS YOU ARE (**NEVERMIND**) – NIRVANA 1991	

35	INSPECTION (CHECK ONE) (**LEFTISM**) – LEFTFIELD 1995	
36	THE BOY WITH THE ARAB STRAP (**THE BOY WITH THE ARAB STRAP**) - BELLE & SEBASTIAN 1998	
37	GOD SHUFFLED HIS FEET (**GOD SHUFFLED HIS FEET**) - CRASH TEST DUMMIES 1993	
38	ENTER SANDMAN (**METALLICA**) – METALLICA 1991	
39	LOSING MY RELIGION (**OUT OF TIME**) - R.E.M. 1991	
40	SONG 2 (**BLUR**) – BLUR 1997	
41	THE ROCKAFELLER SKANK (**YOU'VE COME A LONG WAY, BABY**) - FAT BOY SLIM 1998	
42	OPUS 40 (**DESERTER'S SONGS**) - MERCURY REV 1998	
43	HELL IS AROUND THE CORNER (**MAXINQUAYE**) – TRICKY 1995	
44	REGRET (**REPUBLIC**) - NEW ORDER 1993	
45	UNDER THE BRIDGE (**BLOOD SUGAR SEX MAGIK**) - RED HOT CHILI PEPPERS 1991	
46	THE OTHER SIDE OF SUMMER (**MIGHTY LIKE A ROSE**) - ELVIS COSTELLO 1991	
47	VOODOO PEOPLE (**MUSIC FOR THE JILTED GENERATION**) – THE PRODIGY 1994	
48	WEATHER WITH YOU (**WOODFACE**) - CROWDED HOUSE 1991	
49	FIND THE RIVER (**AUTOMATIC FOR THE PEOPLE**) - R.E.M 1992	
50	DA FUNK (**HOMEWORK**) - DAFT PUNK 1997	
51	LITHIUM (**NEVERMIND**) – NIRVANA 1991	
52	SUPERSONIC (**DEFINITELY MAYBE**) – OASIS 1994	
53	CREEP (**PABLO HONEY**) – RADIOHEAD 1993	

54 SUPERUNKNOWN (**SUPERUNKNOWN**) – SOUNDGARDEN 1994

55 MOTORCYCLE EMPTINESS (**GENERATION TERRORISTS**) - MANIC STREET PREACHERS 1992

56 SCENTLESS APPRENTICE (**IN UTERO**) – NIRVANA 1993

57 RENDEZ-VU (**REMEDY**) - BASEMENT JAXX 1999

58 I AM STRETCHED ON YOUR GRAVE (**I DO NOT WANT WHAT I HAVEN'T GOT**) - SINEAD O'CONNOR 1990

59 TWO PRINCES (**POCKET FULL OF KRYPTONITE**) - SPIN DOCTORS 1991

60 HEY BOY HEY GIRL (**SURRENDER**) - THE CHEMICAL BROTHERS 1999

61 HOOVER DAM (**COPPER BLUE**) – SUGAR 1992

62 HIGH AND DRY (**THE BENDS**) – RADIOHEAD 1995

63 LIFE'S AN OCEAN (**A NORTHERN SOUL**) - THE VERVE 1995

64 ZERO (**MELLON COLLIE AND THE INFINITE SADNESS**) – THE SMASHING PUMPKINS 1995

65 CHICAGO (**VERTIGO**) - GROOVE ARMADA 1999

66 OVER AND OVER (**RAGGED GLORY**) - NEIL YOUNG 1990

67 CRUCIFY (**LITTLE EARTHQUAKES**) – TORI AMOS 1992

68 KOWALSKI (**VANISHING POINT**) - PRIMAL SCREAM 1997

69 HANGAR 18 (**RUST IN PEACE**) – MEGADETH 1990

70 RISINGSON (**MEZZANINE**) - MASSIVE ATTACK 1998

71 YOU COULD BE MINE (**USE YOUR ILLUSION II**) – GUNS N' ROSES 1991

72   LEAVE (**NEW ADVENTURES IN HI-FI**) – R.E.M. 1996

73   BASKET CASE (**DOOKIE**) - GREEN DAY 1994

74   BLACKWATER (**RAIN TREE CROW**) – RAIN TREE CROW 1991

75   WHIPPIN' PICCADILLY (**BRING IT ON**) – GOMEZ 1998

76   AISHA (**THE CONTINO SESSIONS**) – DEATH IN VEGAS 1999

77   SEASONS IN THE ABYSS (**SEASONS IN THE ABYSS**) – SLAYER 1990

78   BIG TIME SENSUALITY (**DEBUT**) – BJORK 1993

79   SPARKY'S DREAM (**GRAND PRIX**) – TEENAGE FANCLUB 1995

80   HENRY LEE (**MURDER BALLADS**) – NICK CAVE AND THE BAD SEEDS 1996

81   BEEN CAUGHT STEALING (**RITUAL DE LO HABITUAL**) – JANE'S ADDICTION 1990

82   GO (**VS**) – PEARL JAM 1993

83   (HURTING KIND) I'VE GOT MY EYES ON YOU (**MANIC NIRVANA**) – ROBERT PLANT 1990

84   HOBART PAVING (**SO TOUGH**) – SAINT ETIENNE 1993

85   HAPPY (**GOOD FEELING**) – TRAVIS 1997

86   BIRDHOUSE IN YOUR SOUL (**FLOOD**) – THEY MIGHT BE GIANTS 1990

87   ENJOY THE SILENCE (**VIOLATOR**) – DEPECHE MODE 1990

88   THERE SHE GOES (**THE LA'S**) – THE LA'S 1990

89   UNSOLVED CHILD MURDER (**AFTER MURDER PARK**) – THE AUTEURS 1996

90   DEMOLITION MAN (**EUPHORIA**) – DEF LEPPARD 1999

91	KILLING ME SOFTLY (**THE SCORE**) – FUGEES 1996
92	THE OBVIOUS CHILD (**THE RHYTHM OF THE SAINTS**) – PAUL SIMON 1990
93	BLUE SKY MINE (**BLUE SKY MINING**) – MIDNIGHT OIL 1990
94	EVERYTHING ZEN (**SIXTEEN STONE**) – BUSH 1994
95	ICEBLINK LUCK (**HEAVEN OR LAS VEGAS**) – COCTEAU TWINS 1990
96	LA GUITARISTIC HOUSE ORGANISATION (**INSTALLATION SONORE**) – RINOCEROSE 1999
97	SMOOTH (**SUPERNATURAL**) – SANTANA 1999
98	PURE MORNING (**WITHOUT YOU I'M NOTHING**) – PLACEBO 1998
99	CANNONBALL (**LAST SPLASH**) – THE BREEDERS 1993
100	GETTING AWAY WITH IT (**ELECTRONIC**) – ELECTRONIC 1991

(75)

BOSTON (1976)

(*More Than A Feeling/Peace Of Mind/Foreplay/Long Time/Rock & Roll Band/Smokin'/Hitch A Ride/Something About You/Let Me Take You Home Tonight*)

Top Track: More Than A Feeling

Listen to the record! These four words were printed on the back cover sleeve to Boston's debut. Evidently, a point was unreservedly being made that here was something worth hearing. Listen to the record! This statement reoccurred in the text recommendation. The band's photograph, however, gave little encouragement for potential buyers. Five grim, bearded longhaireds (with the exception of Tom Scholz - a clean-shaven grim, longhaired), between them looked like they hadn't seen a good time in years. The spirit that spearheaded **Boston** was a passionate love affair with tight harmonies mixed with soft acoustics, painstakingly tuned for an AOR audience. It was released with perfect timing - America 1976.

It's still best remembered for *More Than A Feeling*, a great-in-the-car classic enriched by slick guitars and swirling lead vocals by Brad Delp. Music historians continue to ponder over whether it provided the catalyst, certainly in terms of guitar riffs, for one of rock's greatest anthems. There is little doubt that small resemblances can be heard during the chorus section to *Smells Like Teen Spirit*, but in all other respects the two couldn't be more different. However, there was more to Boston than just the one song.

More successful in their home country, where *Long Time* almost emulated the achievement of their first monster 45, **Boston** was a faultless selection of easy-going pop/rock bursting with instantly lovable tunes. Close on the heels of *More Than A Feeling*, *Peace Of Mind* seamlessly continued with the rejoicing celebration of a warm summer's day mood, with ear-pleasing chords and melodies that made life worth living. Next, the dreamy sci-fi soundtrack, *Foreplay*, created a sense of impending alien presence. Somewhere between mellow Jazz and futuristic atmospherics, tension loomed for a few brief moments then, fading in slowly but surely, hard-stomping *Long Time* restored normal service with a resumption of addictive hooks. The autobiographical *Rock & Roll Band* set up a rocking pace to start off Side 2, a high-flying speed that refused to relent through to *Let Me Take You Home Tonight*. Sandwiched in between were a trilogy of stunners, *Smokin'*, the exquisite *Hitch A Ride* and *Something About You*.

Giving the impression that something from out of this world existed within the sleeve, the LP cover featured guitars disguised as spacecraft travelling towards earth - this was music to set the world alight. Judging by the immediate and long-term sales, the mission was accomplished. For several years it was the most successful debut in US history and it's not difficult to understand why. These days it is unjustly derided by critics, for whom it manifests a side to rock that fails to challenge the status quo. For them, it wasn't helped by being released in such an awkward year, a period of transition when rock music began a long overdue clear out. Paradoxically, for the fair-minded in 1976, it was nice to hear that there were bands that could still make a decent record without resorting to shouting, screaming and spitting.

(76)

THE UNFORGETTABLE FIRE – U2 (1984)

(A Sort Of Homecoming/Pride (In The Name Of Love)/ Wire/The Unforgettable Fire/Promenade/4th Of July/ Bad/Indian Summer Sky/Elvis Presley And America/MLK)

Top Track: *Pride (In The Name Of Love)*

The Unforgettable Fire, its title derived from an exhibition of paintings by survivors of the 1945 atomic bombs on Nagasaki and Hiroshima, was U2's most pivotal record. Concerned that they were being stereotyped as yet another stadium band they re-assessed their musical direction, looking to discover a greater artistic/ambient formula. In Brian Eno and Daniel Lanois they found the dream-ticket co-producers. Gone were the Punk influences so evident on **Boy** (1980) and **October** (1981), gone also the abrasiveness personifying **War** (1983). In came an atmospheric style that brought out the best in The Edge's chiming, jingle-jangle techniques, laying an ideal foundation for Bono's tortured vocals.

Slight traces of the old U2 remained, primarily in lyric and invariably with a specific need to speak out against injustices. On *Pride (In The Name Of Love)* they paid a sincere tribute to the life and spirit of civil-rights martyr, Martin Luther King. Buzzing with Bono's anthemic cries (ironically containing an historical inaccuracy with regards to the time of day that the fatal shot was fired) the lead 45 was an immediate hit. Worshiping the assassinated black icon didn't end with the single, as *MLK* testified. King's vision of a country united in racial harmony may still be some way off but through the words and music of U2 his hopes remain, burning with eternal optimism.

Guilt absorbed *A Sort Of Homecoming* with much suffering taken from the anxious thoughts of another (the track's title was a direct reference to a line written by Romanian poet, Paul Celan). A relative of victims who died in the Nazi concentration camps, Celan was known to be haunted by nightmares caused by his survival – he committed suicide in 1970. The album's opener set a clear objective for the nine songs that followed, where expressing a point of view was paramount.

From the 'hypodermic needle of the album' (according to Bono), *Wire*, through to the echoing, minimal *Bad* (reflecting on heroin addiction) and the experimental nature of *Elvis Presley And America*, **The Unforgettable Fire** was the first full-bodied classic by U2. It observes them at the biggest crossroads in their career. The American obsession hit the jackpot three years later but the initial steps were taken on this often overlooked masterpiece.

(77)

ROBBIE ROBERTSON (1987)

(***Fallen Angel/Showdown At Big Sky/Broken Arrow/Sweet Fire Of Love/American Roulette/Somewhere Down The Crazy River/Hell's Half Acre/Sonny Got Caught In The Moonlight/Testimony***)

Top Track: Fallen Angel

Robertson firmly established his rightful place in rock's Hall of Fame back in the sixties, initially as a backing musician for Bob Dylan, then in his own right as the main composer, producer, lead guitarist and singer in one of the decade's most important groups. A string of highly acclaimed albums followed, but by 1976 it was time for the Band to quit. They signed-off with a career summarising farewell concert featuring performances by a host of musical friends (commemorated on the excellent triple LP ***The Last Waltz***). In 1987, after an absence of over ten years (punctuated by relatively low-key projects), Robertson returned with his self-titled debut solo — it was a long overdue renaissance.

Reading like an A-Z of historic and rising stars, guest appearances abounded. On the lamenting *Fallen Angel* Peter Gabriel contributed vocals to a mournful composition, dotted by religious connotations and a pounding drumbeat that made loudspeakers vibrate. Robertson pondered over whether life had a greater meaning, a significant purpose, in the process making a moving tribute to his colleague from the sixties, Richard Manuel, who took his own life the previous year. It was a long way from the Blues/Country/rock union associated with the Band's earlier work, just a slow-winding, pensive tune, lyrically focused on a melancholic yearning for a sadly missed friend. *Broken Arrow* continued the spiritual theme, speckled by biblical imagery and spectacular atmospherics courtesy of Daniel Lanois and his inspired production.

The real action flowed on the second half. *American Roulette* (featuring Garth Hudson) was a high-speed chase, its uncontrollable pace making it flash by in an instance. A sweeping verdict on the success and downfall of America's popular culture was reached, (James Dean verse 1, Elvis Presley verse 2 and Marilyn Monroe verse 3). The tempo slowed on *Somewhere Down The Crazy River*, the surprise single. The video featured Robertson in romantic embrace with Maria McKee (from Lone Justice), the visual steaminess mirroring the song's sultry huskiness, climaxing with a seductive chorus. Emotions went into overdrive on the final trio - seething anger (*Hell's Half Acre*), contemplation (*Sonny Got Caught In The Moonlight*) and desires for truth on *Testimony*.

Throughout there was the hint of a guiding identity from others; *Showdown At Big Sky* was like the Band at the top of their game, whilst *Sweet Fire Of Love* and *Testimony* contained an authoritative U2 stamp of approval. **Robbie Robertson** was well received on its release (several ***** ratings in the music press) but, with passing time, no longer makes many appearances in greatest albums polls. It is indisputably a benchmark of its time, from a year (1987) when music had hit the doldrums.

(78)

WHAT'S GOING ON – MARVIN GAYE (1971)

(*What's Going On/What's Happening Brother/Flyin' High (In The Friendly Sky)/Save The Children/God Is Love/ Mercy Mercy Me (The Ecology)/Right On/Wholy Holy/ Inner City Blues (Make Me Wanna Holler)*)

Top Track: Inner City Blues (Make Me Wanna Holler)

Motown Records built its empire during the sixties on a foundation of upbeat Soul pitched almost entirely at the singles market. Although rarely moving away from innocent love sagas there was always a belief that, by the time the stylus lifted from the groove, the music would leave you full of life-affirming invigoration. The structures of the 45s varied little, with a continuous succession of masterful treasures manufactured in the Motown production plant - as the adage goes, why change a winning formula? It was a principle ruthlessly exploited.

No wonder that when one of the label's biggest stars, Marvin Gaye, announced he wanted to make an album tackling fiery topics facing modern urban America, there ensued a heated debate. The themes he had on his radar ranged from stricken life in the black ghettoes, drug abuse and concerns for the environment, through to the continuing US involvement in the Vietnam War. Gaye's plans were a major challenge, for not only did they pose a marketing nightmare, there were apprehensions by the record company that he stood on the deck of commercial suicide.

There were concept albums before, but what distinguished ***What's Going On*** was that here for the first time in full provocative glory existed something darker. Whereas the Beatles in

1967 had taken on the identity of a fictitious band, and sang about surrealistic visions backed by a saccharine soundtrack, Gaye touched on real-life troubles. The soulful tunes remained palatable but, in contrast, the lyrics were harder to digest with war, drugs, religion and ecological instability closely scrutinised. These were a series of sensitive subjects that, when combined, resembled a ticking time-bomb – all deeply emotional, with much taken from Gaye's personal experiences.

The title-track drew direct inspiration from contemporary black social flashpoints, whilst *What's Happening Brother* surmised a Vietnam veteran's struggle with adapting to normal life. Notably, many returning soldiers slipped into a lifestyle marred by drug addiction, an unwelcome fact that Gaye acknowledged on *Flyin' High (In The Friendly Sky)*. Years before the rest of us showed genuine concern for the environmental health of the planet, Gaye raised worries on the haunting *Mercy Mercy Me (The Ecology)*. If one thing can be taken for granted, it is that **What's Going On** made us stop and think about the world in which we live, specifically regarding the inhumanity shown to the less fortunate.

That seething resentment, a bitterness fuelled by anger and injustice, began to smoulder on *Right On*, took a temporary respite on the religious *Wholy Holy*, but inescapably the tension continued to expand. It was steering towards an incendiary finish, a storm cloud overhead threatening to unleash damage on a massive scale. *Inner City Blues (Make Me Wanna Holler)* vented the frustrations and alienations of those living in impoverished black areas across the States, spewing a venomous rage. In doing so, Gaye hit upon a repressed truth, namely that contemporary urban America was not the land of equal opportunities.

Motown reluctantly agreed to the record's release. It was a decision that they didn't fret over for too long, with **What's Going On** quickly becoming their biggest selling album in the immediate years afterwards. It was a vital reference point within black music circles, stretching boundaries and showing to the hitherto unconverted, that Soul had more to offer than that paraded in the singles charts. Predictably, this controversial LP didn't initially gain the unanimous approval of the critical establishment. That wouldn't occur until a major re-evaluation of his work following his death in 1984.

(79)

DIRTY MIND – PRINCE (1980)

(*Dirty Mind/When You Were Mine/Do It All Night/Gotta Broken Heart Again/Uptown/Head/Sister/Partyup*)

Top Track: Uptown

Eight songs intrigued by perverse sexuality was a difficult proposition for any record company to handle. For WEA the highly-erotic 'top-shelf' material that Prince offered for his third LP generated concerns about whether it could be released. Fortunately, these rampant slices of sauciness did reach the record stores, for **Dirty Mind** captures the Minneapolis Sound guru setting-off on an ecstatic roller-coaster ride that spanned the eighties.

His raunchy itinerary appeared innocuous on first hearing *Dirty Mind*, powered by a thumping, repetitive disco beat, but Prince's randy lyrics left nothing to the imagination. *Do It All Night* also needed no explanation but respectable, if somewhat strenuous, passion rapidly veered towards deviation. Taboo subjects were 'touched-up', as he sang about oral sex on *Head* (a naughty union with a virgin about to be wed). As if pleasures of the flesh with someone on the brink of entering wedded harmony with another wasn't corrupt enough, straight after came a frantic dance number pumping hard over incest, *Sister*.

Prince's stories intended to provoke a response that's for sure. ***Dirty Mind*** was his early contribution to the creation of the Parents' Music Resource Center, a conservative reaction against suggestive and offensive lyrics. He imaginatively relied on innuendo to paint sexually explicit images, but conclusively it was the mix of funk, soul and disco (best found on *Uptown*) that won him respect. From the opening cut through to *Partyup*, the throbbing fun never let up, dragging the US dance scene kicking and screaming into the eighties. For what it's worth, 'normal' America eventually caught up with this steamy LP, when Cyndi Lauper covered *When You Were Mine*. At a fraction over thirty minutes, short and concise were apt descriptions like the little man himself, but this briefness was more than compensated for by a raucously thrilling buzz.

(80)

A NIGHT AT THE OPERA – QUEEN (1975)

(***Death On Two Legs (Dedicated To ...)/Lazing On A Sunday Afternoon/I'm In Love With My Car/You're My Best Friend/39/Sweet Lady/Seaside Rendezvous/The Prophet's Song/Love Of My Life/Good Company/Bohemian Rhapsody/God Save The Queen***)

Top Track: Bohemian Rhapsody

With dogged commitment to pursue his love for using several genres within the same song Queen's front man, Freddie Mercury, composed an outrageously flamboyant tune that quickly established itself as a watershed in popular culture. Initially there were misgivings by EMI that, at nearly six minutes in length, it was viable to release *Bohemian Rhapsody* as a 45 in an unedited format. Equally, not only was it non-conforming to the radio-friendly three-minutes pop framework, it also felt like something ill-conceived, bolting together segments in a haphazard manner.

Sticking to their guns, Queen bravely released it, unaltered, in November 1975 and the rest, as they say, was history.

On first listening to Mercury's fantastical tale about a depressed, possessed murderer facing execution, many wondered what on earth was going on. More importantly, why was a band keen to make an impression on the rock stage choosing such conflicting musical ideologies (rock and opera) to launch their bid? A ballad-meets-opera-meets-rock-meets-ballad wielded by artistic ingenuity, *Bohemian Rhapsody* required considerable 'growing-on-you' factor before its multi-faceted chemistry was fully appreciated. Saturation media coverage during the final weeks of 1975 went some way towards seeping it in to the nation's conscience.

To assist with the promotion a video was also produced, primarily aimed at TV stations. Consisting of on-stage performances intermingled with silhouette shots of Mercury, Brian May, John Deacon and Roger Taylor, the promo brilliantly complemented the single, showcasing Queen admirably. Their ambition was duly rewarded by a nine-week reign at Number One in the UK chart. Its impact (video and song), however, lasted far longer.

Death On Two Legs spat with ferocious hatred, referring to an unpopular associate as a blood-sucking leech, a sewer-rat. It was clearly not about someone highly regarded (the band's ex-manager took offence and attempted to sue them for defamation). For added impact the lyric sheet left a space after the title, with the words 'Dedicated To…'. Presumably, this gap had names subsequently scribbled in by those in the throes of a despairing relationship. *Lazing On A Sunday Afternoon* (all 67 seconds of it) witnessed Mercury in stroll-in-the-park mood, celebrating an ordinary week that culminated with his favourite chill-out day. Sounding like an old gramophone record plucked from the thirties, it symbolised **A Night At The Opera**, where music not normally associated on the same body of work co-existed in unison.

Love songs are usually written with a person in mind. Taylor's romantic words were saved for a four-wheeled infatuation on *I'm In Love With My Car*, preferring to buy parts for his car than spend time with his girlfriend. The track's growly rock core was at odds with both its previous and subsequent bed-fellows. Re-emphasising the importance of each individual songwriter and upholding meritocracy within the band, Deacon's superb contribution, the bouncy *You're My Best Friend*, was the unexpected follow-up 45. It was simplistic by design and alluringly infectious with its universally identifiable key message.

Arguably *The Prophet's Song*, were it not so long (over eight minutes), was better placed to be the next single. Its rainbow coloured textures ranged from soft acoustics to hard rock, from cold wilderness through to soothing warmth. The vocal canon sequence at the mid-way point was a joy to the ears, more than making up for lyrical inadequacies within this epic song.

A Night At The Opera was Queen's breakthrough LP and early masterpiece. The enormous popularity of *Bohemian Rhapsody*, supported by folksy dreams like *39*, a wonderful and 'genuine George Formby Ukulele' romp (*Good Company*), a charming ballad (*Love Of My Life*) and pulsating rock (*Sweet Lady*), resulted in massive sales but left them with a dilemma taking years to resolve.

(81)

ALL THINGS MUST PASS – GEORGE HARRISON (1970)

(I'd Have You Anytime/My Sweet Lord/Wah-Wah/Isn't It A Pity (Version 1)/What Is Life/If Not For You/Behind That Locked Door/Let It Down/Run Of The Mill/Beware Of Darkness/Apple Scruffs/Ballad Of Sir Frankie Crisp (Let It Roll)/Awaiting On You All/All Things Must Pass/I Dig Love/Art Of Dying/Isn't It A Pity (Version 2)/Hear Me Lord/Out Of The Blue/It's Johnny's Birthday/Plug Me In/I Remember Jeep/Thanks For The Pepperoni)

Top Track: *Isn't It A Pity (Version 1)*

Towards the end, mainly due to disinterest by Lennon/McCartney, plus a growing belief in his songwriting abilities, Harrison received greater freedom within the Beatles to express his religious and philosophical views. Even so, with the advent of his first solo album (disregarding the **Wonderwall Music** nonsense from 1968) it became slightly obvious that he had been stashing away some fabulous tunes (some going back to 1966). **All Things Must Pass** was the culmination of a prolific, creative roll - a triple LP featuring his finest solo work.

My Sweet Lord b/w *What Is Life* gave the Quiet One the significant achievement of being the first Beatle to notch-up a solo Number 1 single - it was nothing short of poetic justice. Spectacular in its immediacy, Phil Spector's Wall Of Sound dynamics levitated the 45 towards Indian religious embracement (including the Hare Krishna mantra) and Western pop values. It remains to this day a hummable anthem that divides opinions down the middle – the easily-pleased that adore its hooks, versus intellectuals for whom it smacked of spirituality's sell-out. Tarnishing his reputation, Harrison ended up on the losing side in a legal dispute over the tune's originality. The courts reached a verdict that it owed a debt to *He's So Fine* by the Chiffons (a US No 1 seven years before his accidental borrowing).

The title-track beautifully reflected his fervent faith, deserving inclusion on the later Beatles records, especially the extravagant **Abbey Road**. Then there was *Isn't It A Pity*, a colossal construction paining over so much wrong in the world. This was an album blossoming with connections to religious quest, undying love and earthly human emotions, from *Hear Me Lord*, *Art Of Dying*, *If Not For You* through to *Behind That Locked Door* and *Beware Of Darkness*. Equally, the music spanned numerous genres - pop, rock, blues, folk and country, with seeming ease. Admittedly, a triple LP was a stretch too far - sides 5 & 6 were nothing more than live jamming sessions, adding little value.

All Things Must Pass was a promising start but a feat Harrison failed to emulate. An extremely sporadic recording output hindered his subsequent solo career, with only the occasional flashes of brilliance to match his 1970 highpoint. Isn't it a pity?

(82)

PARALLEL LINES – BLONDIE (1978)

(*Hanging On The Telephone/One Way Or Another/Picture This/Fade Away And Radiate/Pretty Baby/I Know But I Don't Know/11:59/Will Anything Happen/Sunday Girl/ Heart Of Glass/I'm Gonna Love You Too/Just Go Away*)

Top Track: Heart Of Glass

The commercially most successful group during the period 1978-80 were not Year One punk anarchists but smooth-edged New Wavers, with a knack for crafting perfect pop ditties. Significantly, their lead singer also had connections with the music business going back to the sixties. It was further evidence of Punk's failure to completely eradicate rock's history.

Blondie had already released two albums mildly interesting but, other than the hit 45s, *Denis* (a UK Number 2) and *I Am Always Touched By Your Presence Dear*, there were few indicating signs that their 'difficult' third LP would be so rewarding. **Parallel Lines** appealed on many levels - it was pop, rock and disco, the three populist styles of the times, amalgamated on one extraordinary record.

It began not with a Punk war-cry, but simply the innocuous sound of a phone ringing, followed by Deborah Harry yelling down the mouthpiece, demanding immediate attention. Such impatient urgency set the pace. *Hanging On The Telephone* was cultured pop music (or more precisely New Wave) but, at only 2:17 minutes, complied with Punk standard regulations, whilst moving away from the restrictions of using minimal chords. *Picture This* typified the band's gift for mixing melody with intelligent lyrics, a dream for a teenage generation searching for more than a two-minutes howl. It was the sweetest ode to romance, delivering chic with sufficient abrasion to appease youthful upstarts.

Side Two began with two of the greatest Blondie cuts never released as singles, *11:59* and *Will Anything Happen*. Again, thoughtful words ensured that they distanced themselves from Punk's screaming noises. The two big hits were *Sunday Girl* (a UK Number 1) and *Heart Of Glass* (a US/UK chart topper); both were quality Pop melted by Disco's thumping big-beat and New Wave's impulsive energy. A different version of *Sunday Girl* found Harry switching half-way through to sing in that most romantic language, French. The only regret about **Parallel Lines** was that this rendition didn't make it on the line-up.

Further multi-million selling albums followed but it was in 1978 that Blondie carved out a niche for immaculate Pop confectionery. It was as black and white as that. Fittingly, on the LP's cover Harry pouted at the camera wearing a white dress, whilst the 'backing band' stood like the mafia in black suits and black ties.

(83)

ENTERTAINMENT! – GANG OF FOUR (1979)

(*Ether/Natural's Not In It/Not Great Men/Damaged Goods/Return The Gift/Guns Before Butter/I Found That Essence Rare/Glass/Contract/At Home He's A Tourist/ 5.45/Anthrax*)

Top Track: Anthrax

From the post-war years onwards the dividing line separating the working and middle classes in the UK became blurry, to the extent that arguably there was no longer a distinction between the two. Or at least that's how it was portrayed in school textbooks, by sociologists and the media. Gang Of Four begged to differ with this popular consensus, their debut going to tremendous lengths to pay homage to society's disadvantaged. On **Entertainment!** they made an acute, but deeply incisive analysis of modern urban life. With linear notes referring to a cowboy's exploitation of an Indian, together with three pictures of them shaking hands adorning the LP cover, the band's convictions were in-your-face without even playing the record.

The BBC deemed it too controversial to broadcast on Top Of The Pops and Radio One a song featuring the word 'rubbers', thus with strange wisdom banned *At Home He's A Tourist*. As is so often the case, bestowing such an inflammable status helped fuel public interest. Consequently the 45, together with the neo-Marxist rhetoric album it originated from, came to the attention of more people than it might otherwise have done.

Gang Of Four plundered the depths of despair, unearthing political unrest and wanton exploitation. Beginning with *Ether*, marching onwards to *Damaged Goods*, *Guns Before Butter*, *Glass* and feedback overkill, *Anthrax*, they aligned numerous left-wing anecdotes that made for intense listening.

Originally underappreciated beyond a small core of fans, this album has risen in stature, now rightfully taking its place as an essential British statement. Fulfilling prophecy is rarely achieved in music but **Entertainment!** (or for millions of ordinary UK folk, the future lack of it) sounded alarm bells that the Thatcher years would result in a socially divided Britain - regrettably, few were taking note in 1979.

Owing gratitude to none and complying with a true underground spirit (despite being signed to EMI), there were few concessions to commercial sensibilities. This LP was an attempted victory for the underprivileged.

(84)
CEASE TO BEGIN – BAND OF HORSES (2007)

(*Is There A Ghost/Ode To LRC/No One's Gonna Love You/Detlef Schrempf/The General Specific/Lamb On The Lam (In The City)/Islands On The Coast/Marry Song/ Cigarettes, Wedding Bands/Window Blues*)

Top Track: *Islands On The Coast*

Their debut in 2006, ***Everything All The Time***, although receiving favourable reviews, left a nagging doubt, a sense of underachievement. There were no lingering misgivings on the follow-up, containing ten scrumptious slices of retro pop. ***Cease To Begin***, registering an old-fashioned made-to-measure for LP, sub 35 minutes, continued that déjà vu through to the music, much of which sounded as though recorded eons ago.

One significant factor behind that sentimental, mid-seventies nostalgia was singer Ben Bridwell's similarities with several famous vocalists; Neil Young, Jon Anderson (Yes), Roger Hodgson (Supertramp), together with contemporary influences Jim James (My Morning Jacket) and Wayne Coyne (the Flaming Lips) were all regularly name-checked. In unison with sensational tunes and mesmerising hooks, Band Of Horses struck gold.

Is There A Ghost had few words, but conveyed ecstatic emotion steered on by slick, heard-it-somewhere-before chords and snappy lyrical sound bites. *Ode To LRC* made you realise just how good the world can be, whilst *No One's Gonna Love You* sparkled with unreserved joy, both maintaining an intoxicating brew with mantra-styled, subliminal one-liners. *Detlef Schrempf* awoke memories from the sixties, welded with precision to a dreamy background – Bridwell's scintillating deliverance simply took the entire adventure upwards to a transcendental level.

Islands On The Coast also induced flashbacks, to a different era, this time progressive rock. It was as if seminal synthesiser specialists Yes, E.L.P. and Genesis were unshackled from intellectual restraints, free to 'play' with sound, for sheer fun. It was itching to be let loose, tingling with enticing sensations – a concept lost on those 'serious-minded' bands from the early-seventies that never dared transfer unmitigated happiness to vinyl. *Window Blues* brought the shutters down on a highly satisfying set, with banjos, bluesy guitars, keyboards and Bridwell's angelic performance yielding a modern day gem.

The band's grasp for interlinking tranquillity with impressionable lyrics bordered on exhilarating - those one-liners were impossible to remove from your mind. They left positive, happy thoughts embedded, at a time when groups in general were fixated with a necessity to dwell on wilful misery. In comparison with them, **Cease To Begin** was an abundance of shining gold. In short, if you're in need of a pick-me-up, you should try this.

(85)

RAY OF LIGHT – MADONNA (1998)

(Drowned World/Substitute For Love/Swim/Ray Of Light/ Candy Perfume Girl/Skin/Nothing Really Matters/Sky Fits Heaven/Shanti/Ashtangi/Frozen/The Power Of Good-Bye/ To Have And Not To Hold/Little Star/Mer Girl)

Top Track: *Ray Of Light*

The material girl made a welcome return to form during 1998, the contemplative satisfaction gained from motherhood emerging as a valuable asset in the life and times of Madonna. Notorious throughout the late-eighties due to a series of raunchy videos, she once again demonstrated a unique talent for chameleon adaptation to changing fashions. Using the latest must-have record producer, William Orbit, to oversee her seventh studio album was a blessed choice, his much in demand techniques giving her a badly needed musical update.

Frozen, with its sedate manner and Asian-tinged instrumentation, deceptively revealed little about the mother album, but then came THAT second 45. Showing that she was more than capable of keeping up with trends, *Ray Of Light* was turbo-charged by a quintessential nineties beat that set discos and clubs alive. Much of her hitherto work had conformed to contemporary US dance culture (*Into The Groove, Papa Don't Preach, Cherish*...), hence it was a pure gasp of relief to hear Madge show off stylishly Euro traits.

The title-track wasn't an isolated example of Madonna's explorative push, *Sky Fits Heaven* rocked the b.p.m. to an even faster rate, whilst a decent take on Drum and Bass lit-up *Little Star*. Endearing contentment overwhelmed *Nothing Really Matters* and *Drowned World/Substitute For Love*, all hinting at the profound importance of changing priorities brought about by parenthood. The stereotypical pursuit of weight-obsessed/nerve-wrangled housewives - yoga – was acknowledged with gratitude on the Oriental-flavoured, *Shanti/Ashtangi*, meanwhile philosophical strength defined *The Power Of Good-Bye* with a belief in attaining freedom through letting go. On a powerfully emotional/private album, tiredness inevitably crept in. Fittingly **Ray Of Light** ended with the serene *Mer Girl*.

The former role model for young wannabies was now a woman in her early-thirties embarking on serious parental responsibilities. With nonchalance she became a champion of a different kind, in the name of motherhood. In Madonna's world being a mother didn't signal the end of a woman's attractiveness, if anything, it made femininity more alluring. Absorbing bright, cosmopolitan European disco night life, domesticated bliss, brave new world musical discoveries and an inquisitive search for spiritual reassurance, **Ray Of Light** had many first-rate qualities.

(86)
GRACELAND – PAUL SIMON (1986)

(*The Boy In The Bubble/Graceland/I Know What I Know/ Gumboots/Diamonds On The Soles Of Her Shoes/You Can Call Me Al/Under African Skies/Homeless/Crazy Love Vol 2/That Was Your Mother/All Around The World Or The Myth Of Fingerprints*)

Top Track: *Diamonds On The Soles Of Her Shoes*

Live Aid opened many eyes to the desperate plight of starving Africans. Parallel to the attention drawn by these concerts to the struggle for basic human survival, the entertainment industry led the increasingly public condemnation of the South African Government's apartheid policy. Political isolation, sporting and cultural boycotts also placed a pressurised strain on the regime but, as always, there were some prepared to break from the general consensus.

Paul Simon's career of late had slid on a downward spiral, with little consumer or critical enthusiasm for his recent solo work. Indeed, other than a brief period of class in 1975 (***Still Crazy After All These Years***) there had been nothing worthy of note. During the early-eighties the sixties iconic songwriter became infused by a cassette, ***Gumboots - Accordion Jive Hits Volume II***. With apparent disregard for political correctness, he went in search of its origins, tracing the roots of a unique sound - the mbaqanga (township jive).

Departing from united ranks within the music fraternity, during the spring of 1985 he visited South Africa intent on recording a series of songs for a forthcoming album. Oblivious that contact with black musicians from the country was considered by some to be part of the boycott, the sessions proceeded, only to be met by a predictable outcry. Simon's stance, however, was given a seal of approval from the United Nations Anti-Apartheid Committee.

Their view deemed that his actions didn't contravene the sanctions imposed against the South African administration.

For every annoyed critic complaining about this presumed boycott breach, there were countless more impartial observers that marvelled at Simon's joyous union of African and North American cultures. It was this interaction between geographically separated styles that hallmarked his best work since the infamous split with Art Garfunkel. Disdain over the album's birthplace rapidly subsided, in the process resulting in two hit singles, *You Can Call Me Al* and *The Boy In The Bubble*.

Graceland owed little to the year of its conception and yet now, tracks like *Homeless*, *Diamonds On The Soles Of Her Shoes* and *Crazy Love Vol 2* are synonymous with the era. This was a period when America was engulfed by 'rock' acts such as Bon Jovi, Starship and Fleetwood Mac, whilst Britain remained stuck in a vacuum in the aftermath of the new romantics collapse. At the time, it felt like a dismal period for music, and in hindsight there are few reasons to change this view. This album was a lasting highlight from 1986, a poor harvest year that brings back hardly any fond memories.

(87)
SOUNDING A MOSAIC – BEDOUIN SOUNDCLASH (2004)

(***When The Night Feels My Song/Shelter/Living In Jungles/ Money Worries/Gyasi Went Home/Shadow Of A Man/Jeb Rand/Criminal/Murder On The Midnight Wire/Music My Rock/Rude Boy Don't Cry/Immigrant Workforce/Nothing To Say***)

Top Track: When The Night Feels My Song

Envisage Bob Marley reincarnated, not in his natural Jamaican habitat, but in the cold, snowy land of Canada. Imagine irony too, that arguably Reggae/Ska's finest album in a generation should be originated by a band from Kingston, Ontario! Jay Malinowski (guitar/vocals), Eon Sinclair (bass) and Pat Pengelly (drums) – collectively Bedouin Soundclash – turned in precisely that, on **Sounding A Mosaic**. Picture a sun-kissed beach, thoughts of Reggae unplugged and, ok, consider a joint or two – it perfectly summarises the trio's love for Pop and Ska in a relaxed primal, innocent state, pretence free.

When The Night Feels My Song was the big breakthrough single. Hearing it for the first time, it was as though the Wailers had gained a pop tune within their Rastafarian armoury. *Shelter*, if anything, paid homage to New Wave heroes the Police (check out **Regatta De Blanc**), *Living In Jungles* nodded at Drum and Bass, whereas *Money Worries* respectfully covered the Maytones' hit.

Gyasi Went Home, however, revealed their true template, namely that Marley was the guiding influence, albeit with much of Reggae's electrification stripped away, favoured instead by an acoustic backdrop. The album's most musically sparse moment, *Jeb Rand*, was one to save for the flickering-candle vigils. Echoes of English Punk-poets, the Clash, were audible on *Murder On The Midnight Wire*, but perhaps the highest symbolic track was *Rude Boy Don't Cry*. With an effigy of affluent kids driving expensive cars and listening to musical styles intended for those coming from less fortunate surroundings, it highlighted the spread of 'ethnic' music and its growing popularity amongst the bourgeoisie.

With globalisation shrinking the planet, and multi-cultural societies becoming the norm throughout the western world, it should really be no surprise that albums like this are happening. Gone are the days of pot-smoking Jamaican boys exclusively mastering Reggae, and white dudes turning up the amps for electric guitars finely tuned for heavy rock. In a similar way to the hijacking of Hip Hop by middle-class whites, so it is that Reggae/Ska (instigated by and for the benefit of impoverished blacks) has witnessed an attempted 'take-over' by those not historically associated with its normal environment.

(88)

ENJOY THE MELODIC SUNSHINE – COSMIC ROUGH RIDERS (2000)

(Brothers Gather Round/Gun Isn't Loaded/Glastonbury Revisited/Baby, You're So Free/Value Of Life/Revolution (In The Summertime)/Have You Heard The News Today/Sometime/Melanie/Pain Inside/Charm/Loser/ You've Got Me/Emily Darling/Morning Sun)

Top Track: Glastonbury Revisited

Enjoy The Melodic Sunshine aptly described its contents, as song after heavily-suntanned song showcased a dreamy display of pleasure and happiness. Beginning with the short intro, *Brothers Gather Round*, falling straight from 67's Indian summer skies, the enlightening festivities were immediately apparent. A tantalising sense of déjà vu positively rayed from *Gun Isn't Loaded*, with its striking similarities to early acid rock experimentations. Where had we heard this sound before? Donovan… Pink Floyd…? The album's true purpose went without question by the time its centrepiece, *Glastonbury Revisited*, arrived to harness pleasing acoustics and indescribably beautiful melodies.

One of the all-time great soft Country rock tracks, the band's harmonies borrowed more than slightly from California's favourite surfing sons. Caught up in its swirling beauty, it was easy to forget that this delightful tune name-dropped imageries of running out of acid and love-making under the sun, re-enacting a lifestyle rarely seen since the sixties. It didn't take too long to realise that the journey Cosmic Rough Riders were travelling itinerated a route visiting rock's former masters at almost every opportunity. For *Have You Heard The News Today*, *Morning Sun* and *Melanie* (insert the Beach Boys), for *Baby, You're So Free* and *Loser* (the Byrds and the Hollies circa 1965) and for *Sometime* (sixties revivalists Big Star from their **Radio City** era).

The lyrics to only one song were included (surf the net for the rest) but the attention grabbing was highly justifiable, for *Revolution (In The Summertime)* celebrated the singularly most important thing in life - sunshine. Fuelled by an unmitigated faith in the power of the sun to bring contented happiness, who could fail to be swooned by this?

Everything excelled at reliving the carefree sixties and the real surprise was that, given the death of Brit pop in 1997, it worked like a dream. Simple in its approach, originality of no importance but effective in impact, **Enjoy The Melodic Sunshine** was pure beauty. Every song is a perfect soundtrack for the summer evening beach party. Let the incoming tide trickle through your toes, watch the sun set and allow Cosmic Rough Riders to hypnotise you into a state of absolute bliss.

(89)

BUFFALO SPRINGFIELD AGAIN – BUFFALO SPRINGFIELD (1967)

(*Mr Soul/A Child's Claim To Fame/Everydays/Expecting To Fly/Bluebird/Hung Upside Down/Sad Memory/Good Time Boy/Rock & Roll Woman/Broken Arrow*)

Top Track: Broken Arrow

Undervalued/underappreciated are words freely used these days to describe an artist or an album that has gone unnoticed by the majority. In Buffalo Springfield's case, such sentiments continue to be appropriate. Coming to the attention of the US public in early '67 when *For What It's Worth* reached the Top Ten, a long and productive career beckoned. One of the all-time great protest 45s, it stayed long in the memory but unjustly there were no further big hits. Few people are familiar with their albums, but some of rock's biggest icons started out in this humble group; Richie Furay went on to form Poco, but more importantly Buffalo Springfield marks the beginning of the illustrious recording careers of Neil Young and Stephen Stills.

From 1966-68 they released three uniquely splendid albums but it was on their second, **Buffalo Springfield Again**, where the band's creative forces reached full fruition. Originality seemed low on the priority list at first, with the riff on *Mr Soul* strongly resembling a certain Rolling Stones single from 1965. However, this aside the remainder of this country/folk-rock classic was stunningly innovative. On *Expecting To Fly* Young's voice strained with vulnerable anxiety, whilst enigmatically oozing laid-back serenity. That inimitable characteristic, a nervous vocal riddled with piercing tension, added a fragile tone to the collaged *Broken Arrow* – a thoroughly disjointed batch of segments. It began with a live rendition of *Mr Soul* then edged into a six minutes perilous journey. It stopped and started, stumbled and faltered, had 'bits' bolted on ranging from screaming fans and fairground/carnival samples, and concluded by phasing out with an unnerving heartbeat. Bizarre was the only way to describe Young's first masterpiece.

Not to be over-shadowed Stills provided a down-to-earth balance, albeit his best composition only made it in edited format. Far better was the nine-minutes epic version of *Bluebird* (available on subsequent compilations), that began in a conventional pop vein, progressed towards an extensive guitar solo, then meandered on a voyage that incorporated a burst of 'grunting'.

Buffalo Springfield Again promised so much but failed to launch the band into rock's super-league. Continuous personnel changes contributed to a terminal instability, with artistic differences spiralling so far out of control that their demise was inevitable. As pleasing as a hot summer's day breeze, quality Country Pop such as *A Child's Claim To Fame*, *Hung Upside Down* and *Rock & Roll Woman* will always bring a smile to the face.

(90)

I'M WIDE AWAKE, IT'S MORNING – BRIGHT EYES (2005)

(At The Bottom Of Everything/We Are Nowhere And It's Now/Old Soul Song (For The New World Order)/Lua/Train Under Water/First Day Of My Life/Another Travelin' Song/Land Locked Blues/ Poison Oak/Road To Joy)

Top Track: *Train Under Water*

It began with Conor Oberst narrating for 1:08 minutes, unaccompanied by any instrumentation, the tale of two passengers sat next to each other on a doomed aeroplane. The woman tried unsuccessfully to start a conversation with the gentleman. Mechanical failure suddenly resulted in the pilot making a disturbing announcement, namely that the stricken craft was plummeting 30,000 feet. At this point the man of few words answered the lady's latest question with an incongruous reply. As far as he was concerned it was birthday party time! After an elapsed 1:39 minutes *At The Bottom Of Everything* finally got under way, shifting **I'm Wide Awake, It's Morning** into first gear. It zipped along in a delightful folksy manner, enriched by a mandolin and supporting vocal by Jim James, all brought deliriously to life by a gorgeous chorus. It was the prettiest of starts, but hardly setting precedence for happy tunes to follow.

Oberst came to prominence via the Alternative-Country boom, acknowledged for his visionary story-telling and Folk-ramblings. *First Day Of My Life* and *Lua* added some weighty credence to this but it was the ghost from the distant past that gave his 2005 release its immense grace. Emmylou Harris, by now in her late-fifties, provided a touch of Country royalty to *We Are Nowhere And It's Now*, *Land Locked Blues* and the chug-along *Another Travelin' Song*. Like a matured wine, *Train Under Water* also gave an impression that it was several years old, qualities enthused by superb stringed arrangements set to a surreal ambience.

That old-worldly, nostalgic feeling reached a dramatic finale on *Road To Joy*. This was beauty personified but behind the pleasant exterior lay bitter vengeance, imploding into musical heresy during the album's dying minutes. The controlled harmonies, pristine Folk melodies and purified Country Blues that shined throughout, tumbled amid a throwaway mess-up achieving little, other than a noise. Those that love Country rock with a modern perspective, whilst broadened by historical context, should hurry up and check this one out.

(91)

HOMEWORK – DAFT PUNK (1997)

(Daftendirekt/WDPK 83.7 FM/Revolution 909/Da Funk/ Phoenix/Fresh/Around The World/Rollin' & Scratchin'/ Teachers/High Fidelity/Rock & Roll/Oh Yeah/Burnin'/ Indo Silver Club/Alive/Funk Ad)

Top Track: Da Funk

These Parisians released their debut single under the name Darlin' (inspired by the Beach Boys hit from 1967), but they were not festooned with the same admiration as the Californians, with one British music paper dubbing their music 'daft Punk'. Melody Maker's unflattering remark spurred the duo to use it as the new band name. It fooled many, for Messieurs Guy-Manuel de Homem-Christo and Thomas Bangalter were neither daft or punks.

A bone-crunching dance anthem, *Da Funk*, followed in 1995, driven by a thumping bass that paid respects to seventies Disco, whilst fusing a contemporary, vitalised rhythm. The video focused on the misfortunes of a man wearing a bloodhound mask, hobbling around New York streets with crutches. There seemed no credible meaning to this gripping footage but, in doing so, it set a trend for future Daft Punk promos and live appearances, whereby they seldom showed their faces, choosing instead to hide behind various disguises - bank robber masks, silly glasses and cartoon aliens being the more memorable.

Homework carried on from where *Da Funk* left off. Despite the false start illusion given by the repetitive *Daftendirekt* and the too short *WDPK 83.7FM*, the album began to rock from *Revolution 909* complete with car horns, police sirens and a plea to cease the music. The request fell on deaf ears, as the uproarious crowd continued their party activities. *Phoenix* and the follow-up single, *Around The World*, pounded a course of hard-hitting beats that belonged in a hot, sweaty Parisian nightclub. However, in complete contrast, Carlos Santana playing the axe by the sea was the only way to perceive the alluring, surfed-up joy *Fresh*, with its splashing waves and eternal guitar licks. Pour yourself a cool glass of wine, put the shades on, stretch out on your sun-bed and relax – radiant chill-out music doesn't get much better than this.

Being a techno duo immediately drew comparisons with their English equivalent, the Chemical Brothers, inescapably when hearing the revved-up thuds dominating *Rollin' & Scratchin'*, *High Fidelity*, *Burnin'* and *Alive*. Daft Punk were instrumental in a surge in French bands gaining popularity beyond their own borders, a feat rare in music history. Subsequent releases reached out to the mainstream, via sugar-coated disco pop and futuristic cartoon characters, but **Homework** was their coolest, most varied contribution to modern dance.

Eight of the sixteen tracks exceeded five minutes - ideal for that late night party but, at nearly 74 minutes in length, it pinpointed a growing concern that albums were getting too long. For sure, modern technology brought with it a high level of unwanted cargo. Dreaded 'hidden' tracks and never-ending gaps at the end of a CD – was it absolutely necessary to 'fill' the whole 74 minutes with 'something', at any price?

(92)

MELLON COLLIE AND THE INFINITE SADNESS – THE SMASHING PUMPKINS (1995)

(Mellon Collie And The Infinite Sadness/Tonight, Tonight/ Jellybelly/Zero/Here Is No Why/Bullet With Butterfly Wings/To Forgive/Fuck You (An Ode To No One)/Love/ Cupid De Locke/Galapogos/ Muzzle/Porcelina Of The Vast Oceans/Take Me Down/Where Boys Fear To Tread/ Bodies/Thirty-Three/In The Arms Of Sleep/1979/Tales Of A Scorched Earth/Thru The Eyes Of Ruby/Stumbleine/ X.Y.U./We Only Come Out At Night/Beautiful/Lily (My One And Only)/By Starlight/Farewell And Goodnight)

Top Track: Zero

There was something about the Smashing Pumpkins that singled them out from the hordes of Grunge bands saturating the US rock scene during the mid-nineties. This was still the case even though a glance at the track listing to **Siamese Dream** showed that they were as adapt at compliance as their peers. In keeping with a contemporary trend for one-worded song titles, the likes of *Quiet*, *Today*, *Hummer* and *Rocket* disguised a capability to take Grunge further than merely an outlet for angst-riddled misery. The double CD sequel, **Mellon Collie And The Infinite Sadness**, advanced their philosophy for stretching endurance limits. The latest from Billy Corgan's hyperactive imagination posed a mammoth challenge, with the equivalent of eight vinyl sides.

The instrumental title-track opened this colossal account, creating a misleadingly tranquil setting for the beginning of a 28 track audio feast. Overt seriousness was swiftly swept in, with much soul-searching on the contemplative, orchestral-charged *Tonight, Tonight*. *Zero* had plenty to say during its compact 2:41 minutes - screwed-up rhythms, sneering vocals, sledge-hammer drumming and 100% attitude. Also, spot the half-hearted, apathetic guitar solo, so fitting of the era in which it was recorded.

Familiar Grunge concepts best described the predictable lead single, *Bullet With Butterfly Wings* – it was best forgotten. Greatness, however, was restored on *To Forgive*, stirred on by a haunting electric organ, synthetic harmonies and Corgan's lethargic whimper. A search through rock's quagmires brought out further closet cases, *Love* and *Cupid De Locke*, representing polarised extremes in styles, both defying easy classification. The former felt as though it had witnessed horrors unimaginable, whilst the latter was delicately held together by flickering harps, floating skywards to the heavens. Disc 1 was sub-titled Dawn To Dusk. With so much bleakness heard already, what on earth lay in store on Disc 2 (Twilight To Starlight)?

Hats off to Nirvana - *Where Boys Fear To Tread* and *Bodies* would have made Mr Cobain proud. Next, two cuts owing a nod to the Rolling Stones, *Thirty-Three* and *1979*, so lifelike of their mentors. Sat uncomfortably in between was *In The Arms Of Sleep* swallowing wound-down strings, tearful violins and nightmarish sound effects. No risk of sleep tonight though, *Tales Of A Scorched Earth* could wake the dead and *Thru The Eyes Of Ruby* was too tuneful to blissfully ignore. Disc 2 zigzagged a course underpinned by wildly varying moods - *Stumbleine* charmingly pretty, was offset by *X.Y.U.* soaring the volume upwards. Meanwhile, *Lily (My One And Only)* (or shouldn't that be *I'm Only Sleeping*?) belonged in a parallel universe to everything else.

There were several highlights but the equivalent of four new records in one package took excessive self-indulgence to strenuous levels. Not ideal for one comfortable sitting, but recommended to those with healthy musical appetites, not to mention a determined will-power to see a challenge through to the end. Adventurous definitely, overambitious maybe…

(93)
RATED R – QUEENS OF THE STONE AGE (2000)

(Feel Good Hit Of The Summer/The Lost Art Of Keeping A Secret/Leg Of Lamb/Auto Pilot/Better Living Through Chemistry/Monsters In The Parasol/Quick And To The Pointless/In The Fade/Tension Head/Lightning Song/I Think I Lost My Headache)
Top Track: *Feel Good Hit Of The Summer*

The scale of the expanding gulf between British and American music tastes during 2000 wouldn't be better illustrated than by the upsurge in hard rock in the States. Whereas the UK continued its infatuation with 'bedwetters' the US went heavy crazy – one of the advance party leading the attack were Queens Of The Stone Age, with their second album, **Rated R**.

Taking its cue from the riff-laden formulas prototyped by rock's pioneers, English connoisseurs of more contemporary bands also believed that they could identify the 'ghost' of Terrorvision (listen to *Monsters In The Parasol* to hear why). Assisted by two excellent singles, *The Lost Art Of Keeping A Secret* and the perfectly titled *Feel Good Hit Of The Summer*, sales of the album zoomed upwards (at least in their home country).

Feel Good Hit Of The Summer glorified the drugs culture in its many manifestations, with a repetitive mantra reciting a litany of various substances. It was a sure bet to enrage responsible society but guaranteed to excite bored youth. The buzz of one cut-short guitar solo and a breathtaking run-in to track's end was enough to leave even the most energetic feeling physically exhausted. *The Lost Art Of Keeping A Secret* dwelled happily in between Grunge and a Black Sabbath resurrection of Tony Iommi riffs from circa '73.

Further blasts from the past were noted on *Tension Head* and *Lightning Song*. Meanwhile, *Quick And To The Pointless* screamed for the entirety of its 1:42 minutes, in much the same way that Kurt Cobain had done so on the darker sides to **In Utero**. Likewise, similarities with ridiculed Grunge hijackers, Stone Temple Pilots, left a distinctive mark on *In The Fade*. *I Think I Lost My Headache* was influenced by another guitar chord sequence originally devised by Black Sabbath (*Wheels Of Confusion*) but still couldn't possibly disappoint. In essence, QOTSA summarised rock's many highlights from the last thirty years. With loads of illegality, paranoia and subversion - what more could anyone ask for?

(94)

THRILLER – MICHAEL JACKSON (1982)

(*Wanna Be Startin' Somethin'/Baby Be Mine/The Girl Is Mine/Thriller/Beat It/Billie Jean/Human Nature/P.Y.T. (Pretty Young Thing)/The Lady In My Life*)

Top Track: Beat It

Still only 20 at the time, Jackson's fifth solo LP, **Off The Wall**, was a long overdue career change from a heavily-trodden Motown path. Combining disco pop (*Don't Stop 'Til You Get Enough/Off The Wall*) with enduring ballads (*She's Out Of My Life/Rock With You/Girlfriend*) it prophetically directed towards his mammoth follow-up, **Thriller**. State of the art videos were released in conjunction with the key 45s *Billie Jean*, *Beat It* and *Thriller*, all demanding TV airplay. Meanwhile, MTV maintained its reluctance to broadcast music that didn't constitute 'rock 'n' roll'. However, under growing pressure from corporate giants (notably Columbia Records) the cable channel caved in by agreeing to alter its rigid ideology. Jackson's visuals were crucial in breaking down a colour-barrier that had hitherto complied with a predominant 'white' playlist.

Thriller had something for everyone, effectively becoming a virtual Michael Jackson's Best Of package as hit after hit rocketed up the singles charts (only *Baby Be Mine* and *The Lady In My Life* didn't get 45 status). However, it's easy to say this with the benefit of hindsight, for back then upon the release of the lead single, *The Girl Is Mine*, such high praise was not immediately forthcoming. In duet with Paul McCartney, the song's soulful tones effortlessly scaled the US charts, but appealed mainly to an already loyal fan base. Few appreciated the enormity of what awaited.

Billie Jean was the real calling card. A dance-orientated, disco floor-filler triggered by stunning bass lines, it became an instant classic. In amongst the rapturous grooves there also lay a riveting storyline during which Jackson repeatedly made strenuous denials about being the father of the girl's child. Despite a strong eighties feel it owed much of its rhythmic pleasures to his work with the Jacksons (after they had dropped the 5 tag).

With the inspired choice of Eddie Van Halen to provide the guitar solo on *Beat It* musical genres previously separated began to mix. Was this, as some proclaimed, the opening riffs and beats coming from the sound of the future, with dance and rock in harmony on the same song? For sure, fans that traditionally sat on one side of the divide were now willing to enjoy styles they wouldn't normally entertain. The very same barriers that shamed the early MTV years were being breached at ground level, amongst ordinary music lovers.

The title-track received acclaim in its own right, not just for the top quality dance music, but due to a groundbreaking video showcasing astonishing choreography. Featuring Jackson, partially disguised as a horror movie character, it transformed the relatively novice art form into a serious medium through which to promote music. This and the other awesome videos, however, did not distract from Jackson's party, for the nine tracks on **Thriller** were supreme examples of first-rate pop/disco/soul/rock without a weakness to be found.

From straight-ahead Dance, *Wanna Be Startin' Somethin'*, the housewife-pleasing ballad, *The Girl Is Mine*, to the generous spirit of *Beat It* and *Billie Jean*, every song uniquely contributed to the rise of the Prince of Pop. Achieving this feat with ease, Jackson commanded an authority remarkable at such a tender age. As early as 1983 it seemed that the decade may have already found its most influential album. ***Thriller*** was arguably to the eighties what ***Never Mind The Bollocks Here's The Sex Pistols*** and ***Sgt Pepper's Lonely Hearts Club Band*** had been for their respective decades. In bridging the gaps that kept genres apart, he won over hearts and minds in amongst a wide cross-section of society - old/young, rich/poor and most importantly of all, blacks and whites.

(95)

LED ZEPPELIN III (1970)

(*Immigrant Song/Friends/Celebration Day/Since I've Been Loving You/Out On The Tiles/Gallows Pole/Tangerine/ That's The Way/Bron-Y-Aur Stomp/Hats Off To (Roy) Harper*)

Top Track: *Immigrant Song*

In a brave career move Led Zeppelin, having conquered America the year before by bludgeoning it to within an inch of its life, decided that for their third album they wanted a change in direction. The foundation stones of their success were built upon supersonic, thrusting charges with an emphasis on pushing the noise levels through the pain barrier. To hard core fanatics, any attempt at tampering with this approach was viewed as sacrilege. Nevertheless, the band pressed ahead with their plans, fully aware that they were taking a risk.

After extensive touring, Robert Plant and Jimmy Page retreated to Bron-Yr-Aur, a derelict cottage on the outer edges of Snowdonia National Park. An area of outstanding natural beauty with timeless qualities (rugged mountains and crystal clear rivers), there is no doubt that these relaxing surroundings encouraged the creation of pastoral, Folk arrangements, three of which were included on **Led Zeppelin III**.

There was a predictably varied reaction, with some congratulating the daring shift away from rock, whilst others were outraged by what, to them, amounted to an act of sabotage against the fledgling Heavy Metal movement. Astute fans jumped to the band's defence, commenting that on the first two albums softer shades already existed. The difference this time simply was that the low-key tunes were not camouflaged within heavier constructions.

The headbangers still had their fixes, especially on *Immigrant Song*, a Viking call-to-arms, marshalled by metallic strings. Plant announced the imminent invasion, first with two howling yells, followed by a seismic proclamation of intent. It was all over in just 2:26 minutes but in that time the band systematically defined HM at its very best, launching countless imitators and winning over a new legion of fans. Two further heavyweights, *Celebration Day* and *Out On The Tiles* consolidated their dominant, heavy stance. Sandwiched in between was the seven minutes Blues tour-de-force *Since I've Been Loving You*, with Page transforming the electric guitar into an instrument capable of inducing tears. The real drama though unfolded with the acoustic numbers on Side 2.

Gallows Pole, Tangerine, That's The Way and *Bron-Y-Aur Stomp* connected together almost as one continuous Folk song. The lyrics fell straight from a hippy textbook, particularly on *That's The Way* and *Tangerine*, but this tenderness was secondary to the music's intensity. Who would have thought that gently strummed guitars, built around easy-going countrified melodies, could create as much passion as the skyscraper rock epics synonymous with LZ?

The LP cover copied a growing trend for making sleeves that were more than just a home for the vinyl. A colourful spinning wheel featuring weird and wonderful designs was visible through purpose built holes. Spin the wheel and watch the fascinating, kaleidoscopic images appear – quaint and quintessential of the early-seventies. Years later, Compact Disc buyers missed out on this 'experience', oblivious of the fanciful artwork. The benefits of CD are primarily aural, for looking at a reduced picture of the cover in the jewel case loses so much. Likewise, the original vinyl version included the inscription 'do what thou wilt' and 'so mote be it'. It served as a very public display of Page's increasing, and some felt dangerous, infatuation with cult figure Aleister Crowley. Dabbling in controversial interests only aided in magnifying Led Zeppelin's occultist mystique.

100 GREAT ALBUM TRACKS 2000-08

1. THERE GOES THE FEAR (**THE LAST BROADCAST**) – DOVES 2002
2. THE MODERN AGE (**IS THIS IT**) - THE STROKES 2001
3. I BET YOU LOOK GOOD ON THE DANCEFLOOR (**WHATEVER PEOPLE SAY I AM, THAT'S WHAT I'M NOT**) – ARCTIC MONKEYS 2006
4. VENICE QUEEN (**BY THE WAY**) - RED HOT CHILI PEPPERS 2002
5. FEEL GOOD HIT OF THE SUMMER (**RATED R**) - QUEENS OF THE STONE AGE 2000
6. ONE ARMED SCISSOR (**RELATIONSHIP OF COMMAND**) - AT THE DRIVE-IN 2000
7. ACCELERATOR (**XTRMNTR**) - PRIMAL SCREAM 2000
8. TRAIN UNDER WATER (**I'M WIDE AWAKE, IT'S MORNING**) - BRIGHT EYES 2005
9. DAFT PUNK IS PLAYING AT MY HOUSE (**LCD SOUNDSYSTEM**) – LCD SOUNDSYSTEM 2005
10. IN THE END (**HYBRID THEORY**) – LINKIN PARK 2000
11. BLACK MATH (**ELEPHANT**) – THE WHITE STRIPES 2003
12. UP THE BRACKET (**UP THE BRACKET**) – THE LIBERTINES 2002
13. INTERVENTION (**NEON BIBLE**) – ARCADE FIRE 2007
14. MR E'S BEAUTIFUL BLUES (**DAISIES OF THE GALAXY**) – EELS 2000
15. LEFT BEHIND (**IOWA**) – SLIPKNOT 2001

16	WHEN THE NIGHT FEELS MY SONG (**SOUNDING A MOSAIC**) – BEDOUIN SOUNDCLASH 2004
17	BRING ME TO LIFE (**FALLEN**) – EVANESCENCE 2003
18	GLASTONBURY REVISITED (**ENJOY THE MELODIC SUNSHINE**) - COSMIC ROUGH RIDERS 2000
19	HARD TO EXPLAIN (**IS THIS IT**) - THE STROKES 2001
20	THE FACTS OF LIFE (**THE FACTS OF LIFE**) - BLACK BOX RECORDER 2000
21	CLOCKS (**A RUSH OF BLOOD TO THE HEAD**) – COLDPLAY 2002
22	FLUORESCENT ADOLESCENT (**FAVOURITE WORST NIGHTMARE**) – ARCTIC MONKEYS 2007
23	CELEBRATE YOUR MOTHER (**HORSE OF THE DOG**) – THE EIGHTIES MATCHBOX B-LINE DISASTER 2002
24	IN LOVE (**THE DATSUNS**) - THE DATSUNS 2002
25	THIS IS LOVE (**STORIES FROM THE CITY, STORIES FROM THE SEA**) - P J HARVEY 2000
26	HIGHLY EVOLVED (**HIGHLY EVOLVED**) - THE VINES 2002
27	THE RISING (**THE RISING**) - BRUCE SPRINGSTEEN 2002
28	LIKE A STONE (**AUDIOSLAVE**) – AUDIOSLAVE 2002
29	THAT GREAT LOVE SOUND (**CHAIN GANG OF LOVE**) - THE RAVEONETTES 2003
30	IF I COULD (**IDEAS ABOVE OUR STATION**) - HUNDRED REASONS 2002
31	HATE TO SAY I TOLD YOU SO (**VENI VIDI VICIOUS**) - THE HIVES 2000

32   BLACK SHUCK (**PERMISSION TO LAND**) - THE DARKNESS 2003

33   ISLANDS ON THE COAST (**CEASE TO BEGIN**) – BAND OF HORSES 2007

34   HOUSE OF JEALOUS LOVERS (**ECHOES**) – THE RAPTURE 2003

35   SOMEBODY TOLD ME (**HOT FUSS**) – THE KILLERS 2004

36   HALFWAY HOME (**DEAR SCIENCE**) – TV ON THE RADIO 2008

37   RICH WOMAN (**RAISING SAND**) – ROBERT PLANT/ALISON KRAUSS 2007

38   ON AN ISLAND (**ON AN ISLAND**) – DAVID GILMOUR 2006

39   DO YOU REALIZE? (**YOSHIMI BATTLES THE PINK ROBOTS**) – THE FLAMING LIPS 2002

40   HURT (**THE MAN COMES AROUND**) – JOHNNY CASH 2002

41   SPEED OF SOUND (**X&Y**) – COLDPLAY 2005

42   AMERICAN IDIOT (**AMERICAN IDIOT**) – GREEN DAY 2004

43   VERTIGO (**HOW TO DISMANTLE AN ATOMIC BOMB**) – U2 2004

44   HOTEL YORBA (**WHITE BLOOD CELLS**) – THE WHITE STRIPES 2001

45   WHEN THE SUN GOES DOWN (**WHATEVER PEOPLE SAY I AM, THAT'S WHAT I'M NOT**) – ARCTIC MONKEYS 2006

46   DON'T BE LIGHT (**10,000 HZ LEGEND**) – AIR 2001

47   CHEMISTRY (**ALL ABOUT CHEMISTRY**) – SEMISONIC 2001

48   TAKE THE LONG ROAD AND WALK IT (**THE MUSIC**) – THE MUSIC 2002

49 STARLIGHT (**BLACK HOLES & REVELATIONS**) – MUSE 2006

50 IN THE MORNING (**RAZORLIGHT**) – RAZORLIGHT 2006

51 CHASING CARS (**EYES OPEN**) – SNOW PATROL 2006

52 SOLDIER GIRL (**THE BEGINNING STAGES OF ...**) – THE POLYPHONIC SPREE 2002

53 HEY YA! (**SPEAKERBOXXX/THE LOVE BELOW**) – OUTKAST 2003

54 LEFT SIDE DRIVE (**TRANS CANADA HIGHWAY**) – BOARDS OF CANADA 2006

55 BRING IT BACK AGAIN (**THESE WERE THE EARLIES**) - THE EARLIES 2004

56 A LIFE BETWEEN US (**EVERYONE IS HERE**) – THE FINN BROTHERS 2004

57 SUDDENLY I SEE (**EYE TO THE TELESCOPE**) - KT TUNSTALL 2004

58 YOU KNOW I'M NO GOOD (**BACK TO BLACK**) – AMY WINEHOUSE 2006

59 THE REAL SLIM SHADY (**THE MARSHALL MATHERS LP**) – EMINEM 2000

60 HOPE THERE'S SOMEONE (**I AM A BIRD NOW**) – ANTONY AND THE JOHNSONS 2005

61 TAKE ME OUT (**FRANZ FERDINAND**) – FRANZ FERDINAND 2004

62 BANQUET (**SILENT ALARM**) – BLOC PARTY 2005

63 POOR LENO (**MELODY A.M.**) – ROYKSOPP 2001

64 ROOFTOPS (A LIBERATION BROADCAST) (**LIBERATION TRANSMISSION**) – LOSTPROPHETS 2006

65 THE LUCKY ONE (**NEW FAVORITE**) – ALISON KRAUSS & UNION STATION 2001

66   DRY YOUR EYES (**A GRAND DON'T COME FOR FREE**) – THE STREETS 2004

67   GIMME SHELTER (**TWELVE**) – PATTI SMITH 2007

68   DELIVERY (**SHOTTER'S NATION**) – BABYSHAMBLES 2007

69   VALERIE (**TIRED OF HANGING AROUND**) – THE ZUTONS 2006

70   VIVA LA VIDA (**VIVA LA VIDA OR DEATH AND ALL HIS FRIENDS**) – COLDPLAY 2008

71   JUST A RIDE (**FINALLY WOKEN**) – JEM 2004

72   ROCKSTAR (**ALL THE RIGHT REASONS**) – NICKELBACK 2005

73   CRYSTAL (**GET READY**) – NEW ORDER 2001

74   STAR GUITAR (**COME WITH US**) – THE CHEMICAL BROTHERS 2002

75   REBELLION (LIES) (**FUNERAL**) – ARCADE FIRE 2004

76   TELEVATORS (**DE-LOUSED IN THE COMATORIUM**) – THE MARS VOLTA 2003

77   YOU ARE A KNIFE (**THERE'S A BEAT IN ALL MACHINES**) – VETO 2006

78   CAN'T STAND ME NOW (**THE LIBERTINES**) – THE LIBERTINES 2004

79   BUCKET (**AHA SHAKE HEARTBREAK**) – KINGS OF LEON 2004

80   TIME IS RUNNING OUT (**ABSOLUTION**) – MUSE 2003

81   FORGET MYSELF (**LEADERS OF THE FREE WORLD**) – ELBOW 2005

82   OVER AND OVER (**THE WARNING**) – HOT CHIP 2006

83   THE PRETENDER (**ECHOES, SILENCE, PATIENCE & GRACE**) – FOO FIGHTERS 2007

84	LAZARUS (**DEADWING**) – PORCUPINE TREE 2005	
85	JUXTAPOZED WITH U (**RINGS AROUND THE WORLD**) – SUPER FURRY ANIMALS 2001	
86	SLITHER (**CONTRABAND**) - VELVET REVOLVER 2004	
87	I AM TRYING TO BREAK YOUR HEART (**YANKEE HOTEL FOXTROT**) - WILCO 2002	
88	UP WITH PEOPLE (**NIXON**) – LAMBCHOP 2000	
89	FALLIN' (**SONGS IN A MINOR**) – ALICIA KEYS 2001	
90	MY MISTAKES WERE MADE FOR YOU (**THE AGE OF THE UNDERSTATEMENT**) – THE LAST SHADOW PUPPETS 2008	
91	TODAY'S THE DAY (**LOST IN SPACE**) – AIMEE MANN 2002	
92	TRAINS TO BRAZIL (**THROUGH THE WINDOWPANE**) - GUILLEMOTS 2006	
93	GOLDEN SKANS (**MYTHS OF THE NEAR FUTURE**) – KLAXONS 2007	
94	POUNDING (**THE LAST BROADCAST**) – DOVES 2002	
95	GET UR FREAK ON (**MISS E... SO ADDICTIVE**) – MISSY ELLIOTT 2001	
96	TOO LONG (**DISCOVERY**) – DAFT PUNK 2001	
97	SONG FOR THE RICH (**TWENTYTHREE**) - TRISTAN PRETTYMAN 2005	
98	EVERYBODY'S CHANGING (**HOPES AND FEARS**) – KEANE 2004	
99	BOHEMIAN LIKE YOU (**THIRTEEN TALES FROM URBAN BOHEMIA**) – THE DANDY WARHOLS 2000	
100	OFF THE RECORD (**Z**) – MY MORNING JACKET 2005	

(96)
THE LAST BROADCAST – DOVES (2002)

(Intro/Words/There Goes The Fear/M62 Song/Where We're Calling From/N.Y./Satellites/Friday's Dust/Pounding/Last Broadcast/The Sulphur Man/Caught By The River)

Top Track: *There Goes The Fear*

For those in search of optimism grasped from the jaws of despair, look no further than **The Last Broadcast**. At face value there wasn't an immediate reason for hope, with *Intro* achieving no significant purpose other than to fulfil an obligation suggested by its title. *Words* was comparable to a cross-breeding between the Happy Mondays and Charlatans. Theoretically, a hybrid like this would impose a convincing identity, but somehow the track laboured. Doves were nose-diving to an uncomfortable crash-landing after just two tracks, but then along came eternal salvation.

Triumph over adversity, instilling self-belief from despondency - yes - *There Goes The Fear* was a titanic work that observed a struggled determination to achieve an escapist goal. It wasn't just inspiration gained from the engaging, uplifting lyrics that grabbed your soul but the goliath promise of deliverance generated by ethereal chords. It began with a Byrds styled circa '65 jingle-jangle, before discreetly easing towards flavours more akin to the Stone Roses, culminating in exotic South American rhythms. By song's end (almost seven minutes later) it was like being in another world (or at least, judging by the video, sunny Rio), a freedom attained away from the dreariness of the here and now (presumably, wet and miserable Manchester). Brilliant, awesome, sensational - listen to this epic, again and again, it's the greatest album track of recent years.

It's back down to earth, back to England on *M62 Song* and an adaptation of King Crimson's *Moonchild*. Another short and meaningless instrumental (*Where We're Calling From*) marks time and then we're jetted-off to the Big Apple. *N.Y.* was a schizoid mush, mixing bed-wetting angst with throwing caution to the wind ambition. Better off in N.Y.? Doves would have you believe so. With a silhouette of their previous album, **Lost Souls**, flickering in the background, *Friday's Dust* hovered and lamented over broken confidence. *Pounding* was exactly that and glorious with it, reinforced by do-or-die lyrics. The best foot-stomping track in the world ever!

Given that its title lent itself to the album's *Last Broadcast* had much expectation to satisfy but disappointed. Move on to an absolute treasure, *The Sulphur Man* and rejoice at the chorus, for heaven falls downwards, even with the depressed, yearning vocals speaking of being so close and so far away. **The Last Broadcast** travelled an erratic journey from the nonsense *Intro* through to *Caught By The River* and its closing, pensive thoughts. It was nevertheless, an enthralling adventure that encompassed many musical landmarks. Eclectic is a word used often in reviews but is wholly appropriate on this occasion.

(97)

BLUE LINES – MASSIVE ATTACK (1991)

(*Safe From Harm/One Love/Blue Lines/Be Thankful For What You've Got/Five Man Army/Unfinished Sympathy/ Daydreaming/Lately/Hymn Of The Big Wheel*)

Top Track: *Unfinished Sympathy*

Blue Lines is generally regarded as the best British urban album of all-time. Few realised in 1991, but it was also the first major Trip Hop release, fusing US Hip Hop with a spaced-out drugs culture. It was hard ring-fencing where the centre of gravity lay as Reggae, Rap, Soul and ambient Electronica were cajoled to devise the Bristol Sound.

Definitively British, the video to *Unfinished Sympathy* featured no cheerleaders or flash sports cars, no glitzy lights or colourful streamers, just a drab, urban street. Ironically, the setting was West Pico Boulevard, Los Angeles, with vocalist, Shara Nelson, walking with street-wise intent, showing complete disregard for bikers and drunks along her way. The song's darkness mirrored tensions both within the band and inner-city turmoil at large. Nevertheless, despite brandishing unconventional styles unbecoming of mainstream commercialism, it became a huge cross-over hit, finding approval from a wide expanse of British society.

The cover of *Be Thankful For What You've Got* spanned across the age divide, discovering its resting place somewhere between modern Hip Hop and early-seventies Soul, circa Marvin Gaye. *Five Man Army* echoed Reggae/Ska's influence, *Safe From Harm* a love for *Stratus* by Billy Cobham, whilst pioneering Chill rebounded from *Hymn Of The Big Wheel*, thus concluding arguably Britain's most innovative album since 1977.

Appreciated, at first, only by diversifying hip hoppers, **Blue Lines** is now rightly viewed as an essential record. Laughably, looking back on that era, during the Gulf War the band temporarily had to drop Attack from their name to appease the record label. It showed that music and financial considerations were most definitely no longer separate entities. Even relatively independent bands had to bow to pressure from their paymasters.

(98)
RELATIONSHIP OF COMMAND – AT THE DRIVE-IN (2000)

(Arcarsenal/Pattern Against User/One Armed Scissor/Sleepwalk Capsules/Invalid Litter Dept/ Mannequin Republic/Enfilade/Rolodex Propaganda/ Quarantined/Cosmonaut/Non-Zero Possibility/ Catacombs)

Top Track: One Armed Scissor

After years of innocuous compliance with the politics of Grunge America finally progressed. 2000 gave birth to a badly needed renaissance for attitude-driven rock, with one band in particular providing the catalyst from which much of the new US heavy scene was derived. **Relationship Of Command** contained twelve tracks bursting with fuel-injected power surges that, in many ways, resembled Bad Brains and Fugazi (although the frizzled afros drew comparisons further back in time to MC5). Tense vocals (courtesy of Cedric Bixler-Zavala – sporting the year's wildest haircut) were inflamed by a nervous, at times manic rhythm, serving a blueprint for lyrics pre-occupied with disturbed observations on life.

The opening trio were united by a seamless frenzy of electrifying theatre, peaking with the explosive single *One Armed Scissor*. Travelling with frantic velocity and with astonishing originality of lyric, it was brutally penetrating and yet refreshingly intoxicating, one of post-hardcore's most moving statements. And, as if this wasn't fast enough, what could be said of *Sleepwalk Capsules* in its total 207 seconds craziness?

A break from four successive fireballs finally arrived with the, nonetheless, rampant *Invalid Litter Dept*. Its exploration of the Juarez murders in Northern Mexico, together with a very cautious guitar solo, helped create an uneasiness so fitting of the harrowing subject matter analysed within the lyrics. *Enfilade* (beginning with an unwelcome phone call) searched into the mind of macabre fascination, exposing enforced humility, coupled by a chorus line heralding a rail track sacrifice, an ingenious chant for lost angels.

The first 30 seconds to *Quarantined* offered hope of delicate, tantalising instrumentation to sooth battered nerves but ultimately there was no chance – not with a machete on the loose! *Catacombs* completed what *Arcarsenal* started, with an intensity of freewheeling spirit, the like of which US rock had rarely heard since April 1994.

With lyrics overflowing with thought-provoking stories and continuous musical outbursts filled with rage, there simply wasn't a bad track to be found. Nu-Punk, Nu-Metal, New Wave or just the latest chapter in the revitalisation of where it all began in 1954 with Elvis Presley, whichever way, At The Drive-In were responsible for an album worthy of ranking alongside the legends.

(99)

ELEPHANT – THE WHITE STRIPES (2003)

(***Seven Nation Army/Black Math/There's No Home For You Here/I Just Don't Know What To Do With Myself/In The Cold, Cold Night/I Want To Be The Boy To Warm Your Mother's Heart/You've Got Her In Your Pocket/Ball & Biscuit/The Hardest Button To Button/Little Acorns/ Hypnotize/The Air Near My Fingers/Girl, You Have No Faith In Medicine/It's True That We Love One Another***)

Top Track: Black Math

The best new release during 2003 belonged to a duo from Detroit who, depending on which story you believed, were either husband and wife or brother and sister. Whichever way, Jack and Meg White's **Elephant** was a victory for rudimentary rock where one guitar, drum and singer sufficed. A minimalistic basis for making music in the new millennium was a risky foot-holding, at odds with the over-pampered demands set by modern listeners. Well, in theory yes, but the White Stripes overcame the natural deficiencies associated with raw, fundamental structures, unleashing remarkable songs that felt within easy reach of even the most novice musician.

Seven Nation Army sweltered with the Blues under a scorching Southern delta sky, its bass notes typifying the band's famed trademark for leaving a hook fixated in your head. *Black Math* hit the floor running, its 100% frenetic chaos capturing an anarchic love for care-free fun using electric chords. Just one listen to its late-seventies Punk credentials was sufficient to leave you spellbound.

That déjà vu feeling was unavoidable on *I Just Don't Know What To Do With Myself*. It was, theoretically, infringing on the untouchable, re-working a classic where the original was already clearly definitive. Unexpectedly, by taking the song outside of its comfort zone and wiring it to a garage-band jam, a marvelous execution by the White Stripes added hitherto unknown dimensions.

Using analogue recording equipment helped to envelope a sound that curiously was fresher than anything else released by digital-age enthusiasts during 2003. This was best shown on *Ball & Biscuit*, the album's longest cut, cemented by early HM-meets-Blues and glass-shattering solos. *The Hardest Button To Button* and *Little Acorns* explain why the White Stripes are welcomed in some quarters, whereas sceptics view them as imposters on the rock stage. The latter was initially annoying, with unnecessary narrations at the start but, with the nonsense over, Led Zeppelin riffs and Jack's anxious vocals pushed together, producing high drama. *It's True That We Love One Another* be warned, features Meg sharing lead vocals. After a continuous assault by saturated bluesy tunes and numerous flashbacks to previous decades, it was a whimsical ending, pondering that husband/wife, brother/sister plot.

Traditionalists question the duo's integrity, but there is no doubt that **Elephant** is a giant of the modern age. One thing is also for sure - it will be a talking point for years to come.

(100)
SAILOR – STEVE MILLER BAND (1968)

(*Song For Our Ancestors/Dear Mary/My Friend/Living In The U.S.A./Quicksilver Girl/Lucky Man/Gangster Of Love/You're So Fine/Overdrive/Dime-A-Dance Romance*)

Top Track: Song For Our Ancestors

Steve Miller's partnership with respected producer, Glyn Johns, resulted in a series of first-rate albums during the late-sixties, the best being the much-overlooked **Sailor**. It began with a track that can only be described as one of the finest instrumentals ever. Listening to *Song For Our Ancestors* it's almost possible to smell the salty sea air and feel the breeze coming in from the ocean. It's made even more realistic by a foghorn blowing from a ferry boat in the harbour and the sound of splashing waves. For close on six wonderful minutes it never fails to stimulate thoughts of an aquatic adventure.

Fundamentally Miller, born in Milwaukee, Wisconsin, aimed for an American sound. Proud of his musical heritage he certainly was, as tracks like the harmonica-textured *Living In The U.S.A.* revealed. His second LP was blessed by the traditional Blues of America's past, with acoustic and slide guitars also present on the upbeat numbers, *Gangster Of Love* and *Overdrive*. The second best highlight on **Sailor** (few songs on any record can top *Song For Our Ancestors*) was the assortment of styles rolled into one, *Lucky Man*. With similarities to the Band and Cream through to mild traces of the Byrds, it lasted barely three minutes but felt like it could have benefited from a further five.

Pointing towards the futuristic visions of his work during the mid to late-seventies, *Quicksilver Girl* showed Miller's instinctive sense of harmony and semi-Beach Boys parody. In contrast to the album's sublime beginnings, *Dime-A-Dance Romance* positively rocked, making for an unsettling finale to an enigmatic set.

The Space Cowboy's unique adaptation of historical American styles failed to translate into hard sales. It wouldn't be until 1973 when he reinvented himself as one of the champions of AOR that Miller reaped the recognition that his music warranted.

THE GREATEST ALBUMS YEAR-BY-YEAR

1965	**HIGHWAY 61 REVISITED** – BOB DYLAN
1966	**REVOLVER** – THE BEATLES
1967	**SGT PEPPER'S LONELY HEARTS CLUB BAND** – THE BEATLES
1968	**ASTRAL WEEKS** – VAN MORRISON
1969	**ABBEY ROAD** – THE BEATLES
1970	**BRYTER LAYTER** – NICK DRAKE
1971	**LED ZEPPELIN IV**
1972	**EXILE ON MAIN STREET** – THE ROLLING STONES
1973	**DARK SIDE OF THE MOON** – PINK FLOYD
1974	**GRIEVOUS ANGEL** – GRAM PARSONS
1975	**BLOOD ON THE TRACKS** – BOB DYLAN
1976	**BOSTON**
1977	**NEVER MIND THE BOLLOCKS HERE'S THE SEX PISTOLS** – SEX PISTOLS
1978	**PARALLEL LINES** - BLONDIE
1979	**UNKNOWN PLEASURES** – JOY DIVISION
1980	**CLOSER** – JOY DIVISION
1981	**COMPUTER WORLD** – KRAFTWERK
1982	**THRILLER** – MICHAEL JACKSON
1983	**SWORDFISHTROMBONES** – TOM WAITS
1984	**BORN IN THE U.S.A.** – BRUCE SPRINGSTEEN
1985	**PSYCHOCANDY** – THE JESUS AND MARY CHAIN
1986	**GRACELAND** – PAUL SIMON
1987	**THE JOSHUA TREE** – U2

1988	**GREEN** – R.E.M.	
1989	**DOOLITTLE** - PIXIES	
1990	**RAGGED GLORY** – NEIL YOUNG	
1991	**NEVERMIND** - NIRVANA	
1992	**AUTOMATIC FOR THE PEOPLE** – R.E.M.	
1993	**IN UTERO** - NIRVANA	
1994	**DEFINITELY MAYBE** - OASIS	
1995	**THE BENDS** - RADIOHEAD	
1996	**EVERYTHING MUST GO** – MANIC STREET PREACHERS	
1997	**OK COMPUTER** - RADIOHEAD	
1998	**MOON SAFARI** - AIR	
1999	**THE CONTINO SESSIONS** – DEATH IN VEGAS	
2000	**THE FACTS OF LIFE** – BLACK BOX RECORDER	
2001	**IS THIS IT** – THE STROKES	
2002	**THE RISING** – BRUCE SPRINGSTEEN	
2003	**ELEPHANT** – THE WHITE STRIPES	
2004	**SOUNDING A MOSAIC** – BEDOUIN SOUNDCLASH	
2005	**I'M WIDE AWAKE, IT'S MORNING** – BRIGHT EYES	
2006	**WHATEVER PEOPLE SAY I AM, THAT'S WHAT I'M NOT** – ARCTIC MONKEYS	
2007	**NEON BIBLE** – ARCADE FIRE	
2008	**DEAR SCIENCE** – TV ON THE RADIO	

THE GREATEST TRACKS YEAR-BY-YEAR

1965   LIKE A ROLLING STONE (**HIGHWAY 61 REVISITED**) – BOB DYLAN

1966   TOMORROW NEVER KNOWS (**REVOLVER**) – THE BEATLES

1967   THE END (**THE DOORS**) – THE DOORS

1968   ASTRAL WEEKS (**ASTRAL WEEKS**) – VAN MORRISON

1969   MIDNIGHT RAMBLER (**LET IT BLEED**) – THE ROLLING STONES

1970   SOUTHERN MAN (**AFTER THE GOLD RUSH**) – NEIL YOUNG

1971   STAIRWAY TO HEAVEN (**LED ZEPPELIN IV**) – LED ZEPPELIN

1972   WILLIN' (**SAILIN' SHOES**) – LITTLE FEAT

1973   TIME (**DARK SIDE OF THE MOON**) – PINK FLOYD

1974   RETURN OF THE GRIEVOUS ANGEL (**GRIEVOUS ANGEL**) – GRAM PARSONS

1975   BORN TO RUN (**BORN TO RUN**) – BRUCE SPRINGSTEEN

1976   I WISH (**SONGS IN THE KEY OF LIFE**) – STEVIE WONDER

1977   ANARCHY IN THE UK (**NEVER MIND THE BOLLOCKS HERE'S THE SEX PISTOLS**) - SEX PISTOLS

1978   TAKE ME TO THE RIVER (**MORE SONGS ABOUT BUILDINGS AND FOOD**) – TALKING HEADS

1979   LONDON CALLING (**LONDON CALLING**) – THE CLASH

1980	ATROCITY EXHIBITION (**CLOSER**) - JOY DIVISION
1981	COMPUTER LOVE (**COMPUTER WORLD**) – KRAFTWERK
1982	THE MESSAGE (**THE MESSAGE**) – GRANDMASTER FLASH & THE FURIOUS FIVE
1983	BLUE MONDAY (**POWER, CORRUPTION & LIES**) – NEW ORDER
1984	WHAT DIFFERENCE DOES IT MAKE? (**THE SMITHS**) – THE SMITHS
1985	YOU TRIP ME UP (**PSYCHOCANDY**) – THE JESUS & MARY CHAIN
1986	SLEDGEHAMMER (**SO**) – PETER GABRIEL
1987	WELCOME TO THE JUNGLE (**APPETITE FOR DESTRUCTION**) – GUNS N' ROSES
1988	WORLD LEADER PRETEND (**GREEN**) – R.E.M.
1989	DEBASER (**DOOLITTLE**) – PIXIES
1990	STEP ON (**PILLS 'N' THRILLS AND BELLYACHES**) – HAPPY MONDAYS
1991	SMELLS LIKE TEEN SPIRIT (**NEVERMIND**) – NIRVANA
1992	CONNECTED (**CONNECTED**) – STEREO MCS
1993	DISARM (**SIAMESE DREAM**) – THE SMASHING PUMPKINS
1994	ROCK 'N' ROLL STAR (**DEFINITELY MAYBE**) – OASIS
1995	STREET SPIRIT (FADE OUT) (**THE BENDS**) – RADIOHEAD
1996	A DESIGN FOR LIFE (**EVERYTHING MUST GO**) – MANIC STREET PREACHERS
1997	BITTER SWEET SYMPHONY (**URBAN HYMNS**) – THE VERVE
1998	LA FEMME D'ARGENT (**MOON SAFARI**) – AIR

1999	THE BARTENDER AND THE THIEF (**PERFORMANCE AND COCKTAILS**) – STEREOPHONICS
2000	FEEL GOOD HIT OF THE SUMMER (**RATED R**) – QUEENS OF THE STONE AGE
2001	THE MODERN AGE (**IS THIS IT**) – THE STROKES
2002	THERE GOES THE FEAR (**THE LAST BROADCAST**) – DOVES
2003	BLACK MATH (**ELEPHANT**) – THE WHITE STRIPES
2004	WHEN THE NIGHT FEELS MY SONG (**SOUNDING A MOSAIC**) – BEDOUIN SOUNDCLASH
2005	TRAIN UNDER WATER (**I'M WIDE AWAKE, IT'S MORNING**) – BRIGHT EYES
2006	I BET YOU LOOK GOOD ON THE DANCEFLOOR (**WHATEVER PEOPLE SAY I AM, THAT'S WHAT I'M NOT**) – ARCTIC MONKEYS
2007	INTERVENTION (**NEON BIBLE**) – ARCADE FIRE
2008	HALFWAY HOME (**DEAR SCIENCE**) – TV ON THE RADIO

... And Finally

The advent of the internet and specifically the resultant ability to download music, usually for free, means that the concept of an album currently faces its biggest challenge. Gone are the days when a stereotypical record collector makes their purchases in a local store. Nowadays, it's more a case of staring at the computer monitor screen listening to 'streamed' songs, clicking a mouse and cherry-picking individual tracks.

Already a new generation smirk at the idea that people listened to a complete body of work on one CD. Perish their thoughts on vinyl, for yes, we really did (some still do) enjoy music via a 12 inch circular, black piece of plastic with a hole in the middle. To play this antique we delicately lowered a stylus (known as a needle) down on to the vinyl rotating on a turntable. Yes true also, if the stylus was not respected with the utmost care it left irreparable scratches on the disc. It was infuriating when this occurred but, man, it was a way of life, and we would not have wanted it any other way.

The faithful album plays an unsung factor - providing stability in a turbulent world. Records we enjoyed thirty years ago remain loyal companions in our private universe, taking pride of place in the home. They are too important to be thrown out during those spontaneous moments of clearing out the clutter. Can we say where friends and work mates from decades ago are now? Most likely not, yet the albums we bought all those years ago are still with us. Such is the way of modern times, we get married, have children, divorce, re-marry, continually change jobs and move homes, and all the time our album collection stays a constant friend.

The very word 'album' has remained unchallenged despite the emergence of cassette, CD, Mini Disc and MP3. The word still suffices to adequately describe the contents, regardless of the format on which it is played. There are, however, troublesome times ahead, with its concept possibly soon to be viewed as a relic, taking its place alongside vinyl, the gramophone and the reel-to-reel tape recorder. If that moment comes, it will be a sad day for popular entertainment. Admittedly, it's going to be a gradual process, beginning already with the download/I-Pod lovers cherishing their hand-picked playlists. For now, at least, we can be thankful for the huge variety of albums we've worshipped over the years and live in hope that many more are still to come.

ABOUT THE AUTHOR

Andrew Southwood's love affair with music began in 1973, with the purchase of his first 45. In 1975 he moved on to the big world of albums, resulting in a passion that has stayed with him ever since. He is an enthusiastic writer, devoted father and husband, residing in Wiltshire, United Kingdom.

www.ingramcontent.com/pod-product-compliance
Ingram Content Group UK Ltd.
Pitfield, Milton Keynes, MK11 3LW, UK
UKHW041439180426
11947UKWH00007B/521